The Ghosts of Charlottesville and Lynchburg

... and nearby environs

by L. B. Taylor, Jr.

Photographs by the Author
Illustrations by Brenda E. Goens

ISBN-0-9628271-6-9

Contents

Acknowledgements

As with my other ghost books, many, many people contributed generously and graciously to the making of "The Ghosts of Charlottesville and Central Virginia." I am indebted to all those who shared their personal experiences with me, as well as to those who helped in the research.

No such list is ever complete and forgive me for memory lapses, but I would like to especially thank the wonderful people at the following libraries: Alderman at the University of Virginia; Charlottesville Public; Waynesboro; Staunton; Jones Memorial in Lynchburg; Lynchburg Public; Harrisonburg Public; William & Mary; and Williamsburg.

Thanks, too, to: the ladies at the Charlottesville Visitors Center; Mrs. Diane Carr of Montpelier (Miss Minnie); Betty Langhorne (Tallwood); Jack Deaton (Jerdone's Castle); Jim and Suzanne Elmore (Tufton); Nancy Connor, Estelle and Arthur Stevens, and Joyce Stevens (Proffitt House); Ella Hanson (Mountain View); Bill Edwards (Swannanoa); Charles Culbertson (Selma and the Ghost Hotel); Meg Hibbert (several houses in Amherst County); and J. B. Yount III of Waynesboro (Stonewall Cottage).

Author's Personal Note

Here we go again! Wow, three books in three years! "The Ghosts of Tidewater" in 1990, "The Ghosts of Fredricksburg" in 1991, and now "The Ghosts of Charlottesville, Lynchburg and Nearby Environs." I must have a masochistic bent. But I couldn't resist. The reception to my other books has been so kind, the people have been so nice, and the travel and interviewing have been so interesting.

The letters keep coming in from all over. I should know better by now, but I continue to be amazed at the deep interest people take in psychic phenomena. This past year, for instance, I met a lady who started up a nightly ghost tour in Williamsburg. She based the tour on my book, "The Ghosts of Williamsburg," which was published in 1983. She said more than 2,000 people took it last summer alone. When the Fredricksburg book came out, I did a local television show there, and some autograph signing. It was fun.

Critics were gracious in their reviews, too. And recently, I was surprised to learn that Fate Magazine had done a write-up. I was surprised because I had not sent them a copy. I just have to quote from David Godwin's review: "Most privately printed books have a fairly amateurish appearance. Despite the author's writing talent (or lack of it), he or she generally has little or no knack for typography, layout, or book production.

"The Ghosts of Fredricksburg" is a wonderful exception. . . The tales are told in a simple and straightforward manner that is nevertheless entertaining, at times even spellbinding. . . This is a good and entertaining read for the casual browser as well as the serious student."

Who am I to argue?

It seemed only natural to swing down from Fredericksburg to the Charlottesville-Lynchburg area. This is, after all, the land of giants — Jefferson, Madison, Monroe, Lee, and Jackson, among many others. But more on the region in the introduction. There was a very personal satisfaction in doing this book. My roots are here. The Taylors in my ancestry settled in Amherst County, and my grandfather, John Samuel Taylor, married Lula James Barbour. The Barbours are scattered throughout Central Virginia. So in tracking the backroads and byways of this part of the state, I was, in effect, coming home. I am a native of Lynchburg. The hours I spent there, walking the historic streets, and poring over dusty volumes and yellowed documents at the Jones Memorial Library were both pleasant and fruitful.

From mountaintop to valley depth, I was greeted with the cordial hospitality of which Central Virginians, inspired by Jefferson at Monticello, are famous.

I can still vividly remember, as a skinny, freckle-faced, red-headed kid half a century ago, sitting on the porch steps of my grandfather's farmhouse in the warm summer evenings and with a gentle breeze blowing — listening with my cousins to my Uncle Jack as he told his famous ghost stories. What a wonderful time-honored tradition we have all but lost to the age of television! We were fascinated. And when Uncle Jack's voice would trail off to no more than a whisper at the climax of the tale, and then he would suddenly jump up and grab one of us, we were scared out of our wits! I can remember one night in particular. I had been sent to bed upstairs, by myself, in a darkened back bedroom. The images of my Uncle's ghosts and goblins were swirling in my head, and when something banged into the screen over the open window and made a loud thud, I thought my heart would stop. It was probably just a huge bug, but to me the devil himself was out there!

And I will never, ever forget the night when I was there at the old farm — I must have been about 10 — and my father said he would give me a dollar if I would walk back up to the barn, then onto the country dirt road, down toward the creek, and back up the rocky driveway past the thick briar patches to the house. It was probably a walk of a mile and half or perhaps two. In those days, a dollar would buy a lot of candy, so I eagerly accepted. Plus I didn't want any of my elders to think I was afraid.

It had to be the longest walk of my life. There was reputed to be a headless horseman who rode down the old road on moonlit nights. And there was no telling how many wild animals were lurking in my path. But I started out nevertheless. Before I even got to the barn, I could feel the hair on the back of my neck rise when a rabbit — or something — shot across the lane right in front of me. Along the back road, I whistled as loudly as I could, and somehow I managed to make the long loop with no further incidents other than what my own mind had conjured up. Sometime later, my dad told me he had cut through the cow pasture and was waiting for me down on the country road. He had planned to jump out and scare me, but he said when he saw me, my eyes were so big, he just didn't have the heart to do it.

What sweet memories!

* * * * *

I am indebted to my cousin, Layton Taylor, proprietor of the T &
W convenience store on state Route 671, just off highway 29, a little
north of Monroe (eight miles north of Lynchburg), for sharing a psychic experience or two he had in the area. Well, to be exact, he is like
me. He didn't have a direct experience, but it was close. Layton's
maternal grandmother, Nora Fortune Bibb, owned a house named
Windridge, built around 1902. It is near Greenfield, between
Wintergreen and Afton Mountain. Layton inherited the house some
years ago, refurbished it, and hopes to move there in his retirement
years. He says he finds a "tremendous sense of comfort there." This
is the rule, but there have been exceptions.

On one occasion, David Hammock, a friend of my cousin's went
to the house to do some electrical work. Layton picks up the story:
"He said he had about two days work there, so I was surprised to see
him back in my store the next morning. I asked him what happened.
He said when he got to Windridge, which admittedly is in a rather
isolated area, as soon as he walked in the front door he smelled the
strong aroma of fresh brewed coffee. He thought maybe another
workman was at the house, and he went to the kitchen where the
smell was the strongest, but there was no one else there and no coffee brewing or otherwise. Later on, he turned all the power off in the
house and was repairing a light in my grandfather's room upstairs.
He screwed in a new light bulb, and as he climbed down off the ladder, he looked up, and the light bulb was *on*! He rushed downstairs
to check the master switch again, and the *power was still off*! That was
why he had come back early."

The other occasion when something very strange happened at
my cousin's house occurred a few years ago when he took some
friends over to show them the place. They had brought along
another man, who Layton did not know. Again, let him tell the story:
"Did you ever see someone who you immediately took a dislike to?
Well, that's what happened to me. There was just something about
this person that rubbed me wrong. Anyway, when we got to the
house, this fellow charged right in ahead of the rest of us. He went to
the back of the house. We didn't think anything of it, particularly,
and were standing in one of the front rooms, when, about a minute
or two later, he came running through he house and bolted outside,
screaming as loud as he could scream.

"Something obviously had scared the hell out of him. There was
no mistaking the fact that the was definitely *not* pretending! After a
while, when he had calmed down, he told us what had happened.

He had found a trap door in the rear of the house. It leads to an old root cellar. He said he had opened the trap door, and saw an old woman wearing gold rimmed spectacles and a black dress, with her silver-gray hair rolled up in a bun. He had perfectly described my grandmother, who had been dead for 40 years! There is no way he could have had any previous knowledge of who she was or what she looked like.

"No amount of persuasion could convince him to set foot back in the house. The rest of us then did go back to the root cellar and we lifted the trap door. We didn't see anything, but the cellar was frigid, and this was in the summer. I couldn't explain that. Curiously, the man who claimed he had seen my grandmother was stabbed to death at a party exactly one year to the day after we had gone to the house."

Maybe my cousin Layton will let me sleep over there sometime after he retires and we can both have a chance to experience our first psychic experience. Meanwhile, I dedicate this book to him.

* * * * *

And then there is the funny side of ghost writing. A few months ago, I appeared on a radio show about psychic phenomena with the Reverend Richard (Dick) Hughes Carter of Williamsburg, a walking encyclopedia on local lore. Rev. Carter told the following true anecdote: Seems one day in the winter, five Colonial Williamsburg historical interpreters, all women, were driven out to St. Peters Episcopal Church in New Kent County one afternoon for a tour of the facilities and a briefing on the history of the church. The ladies were all dressed in the traditional colonial costumes, covered with hooded capes, since the weather was a bit nasty.

As they left the church late in the afternoon, a mist was rising in the darkening gloom. The ladies pulled their hoods up over their heads and sat down on a bench to await their ride back to Williamsburg. The bench was next to the church cemetery. Soon they heard a vehicle approaching, and assuming this was their driver, the ladies arose from the bench. However, it was not their driver. It was a tourist from New Jersey who apparently was lost. From the road, in the rising mist, he saw five hooded figures in colonial costume suddenly appear out of nowhere, among the towering tombstones. The ladies said the man let out an audible gasp, slammed his foot on the accelerator, and promptly drove into a tree! He then backed up and sped off, spinning his tires, without even bothering to stop and see what damage he had done to his car.

Introduction

"His presence is still felt here." . . . That is how one visitor's brochure describes the dominating, pervasive influence — nearly 170 years after his death — that Thomas Jefferson exerts to this day over Charlottesville, Albemarle County, and Central Virginia. In American history, this broad area sweeping west to Staunton and Lexington, south to Lynchburg and Bedford, east through Louisa, Fluvanna and Goochland Counties, and north from Harrisonburg to Montpelier — is truly the land of giants. It is the land of Jefferson, Madison, Monroe, Patrick Henry, Robert E. Lee, Thomas "Stonewall" Jackson, Lewis & Clarke, Woodrow Wilson, and so many others.

Here, in the foothills of the Blue Ridge Mountains, natural beauty and colorful legend peacefully co-exist. Amidst the rolling hills and fertile valleys are literally hundreds of grand manor homes, flanked by flowering dogwoods and aromatic boxwoods, many of them dating to the 18th century. Here is Monticello, Ash Lawn, Michie Tavern, Castalia, Tallwood, and Castle Hill, all in the vicinity of what has been called "the fairest Georgian City of the New World." Down Route 29, an hour's drive away, is the storied Diamond Hill district of rustic Lynchburg and street after street of classic ante-bellum mansions.

It is a land soaked with the blood of Revolutionary War patriots and the heroic young men who gave their lives for their cause in the War Between the States. In such a region so rich in its historical heritage, it is no wonder, then, that an aura of psychic phenomena hangs as thick and as encompassing as the early morning fog. Central Virginia truly teems with ghosts, and the range of spectral manifestations is so broad and so bizarre as to thoroughly intrigue, and at times amaze, even the most jaded follower of psychical happenings.

It is here, in Augusta County, that one of the most profound and most well documented cases of incredible poltergeist activity in recorded history occurred at a simple farmhouse in the 1820s. Here, too, near Charlottesville, is the site of the legendary Moon Ghost of Scottsville who wreaked terrifying havoc over a two year period in the 1860s. Here, in the shadows of the mountains is the mythical-yet-true tale of the enormous apparitional dog who guarded the grave of his long-dead master; and of the albino beasts of Montpelier. In Lynchburg, old-timers still talk about the extraordinary self-rocking cradle; a phenomenon attested to by hundreds of eye witnesses. Near Bedford, scores of fortune seekers still dig for a fabled treasure allegedly buried 170 years ago. There are supernatural ties to the famous — to Sarah Henry, Patrick Henry's mother, at Winton; to James Monroe at Ash Lawn; and, perhaps, even to the Sage of Monticello, Jefferson himself. There are vivid accounts of sadness, lost loves, and tragedy; of hangings and burnings, murders and shootings, and the spirits such traumatic occurrences left behind. And there is serenity, and peace, and the passing of ethereal beings into the "Other World." There is, in short, a psychic cornucopia of strange events that will test the nerve and defy the imagination.

* * * * *

What exactly is a ghost? I have addressed this question sparingly in each of my previous books on regional Virginia hauntings. The definitive answer, if there is one, appears still as nebulous and transparent as the wraith-like apparitions of spirits themselves. Experts have offered many questionable definitions: "A disembodied soul . . . the soul of a dead person believed to be the inhabitant of the unseen world, or to appear to the living in bodily likeness . . . a surviving emotional memory of someone who has died traumatically, and usually tragically, but is unaware of his or her death . . . something from human personality that exists after death . . . a form of psychic energy which manifests itself over a period of time, most often in one place . . ."

Historically, ghosts have been written about since at least the fourth century BC, when the Greek philosopher Plato wrote of "the soul which survives the body." Plato said this soul sometimes is wrapped in an "earth covering, which makes it heavy and visible, and drags it down to the visible region . . . And thus these wandering souls haunt, as we call it, the tombs and monuments of the dead, where such phantoms are sometimes seen." Four hundred years ago, Frenchman Pierre Le Loyer penned: "There are plenty of houses haunted by these spirits and goblins, which ceaselessly disturb the sleep of those who dwell in them. They will stir and overturn the utensils, vessels, tables, boards, dishes, bowls . . . throw stones, enter chambers . . . pull the curtains and coverlets, and perpetuate a thousand tricks."

Some psychical experts contend that spirits are filmy afterimages of particularly strong feelings and portentous events. In 1908, British physicist Sir Oliver Lodge proposed that spectral phenomena was a "ghostly representation of some long past tragedy." . . . that violent emotions might somehow imprint themselves on their environment for later transmission to people sensitive enough to "tune them in."

Many spiritualists believe that the soul leaves the body at death, but under certain circumstances "it" may tarry on earth instead of proceeding to the "other side" and thus be observed as a ghost. Ernesto Bozzano, an Italian psychical researcher, theorized that apparitions were not the souls of the dead, but rather telepathic messages from their lingering bodiless minds which have many of the characteristics usually attributed to spirits. And American parapsychologist William G. Roll has written that stored psychic traces from the past can evoke apparitions; that in many cases a person's mental state plays an active role, unconsciously creating haunting phenomena to satisfy emotional needs. Others have said ghostly phenomena depends on the emotional force of the original psychic "imprint" and the sensitivity of the recipient.

And on and on. I like the simple explanation offered by Oxford University Professor Henry Habbeley Price. He said such phenomena exists "in a dimension or dimensions unknown to us."

Are ghosts real? It is a time honored question. Are the reports of mysterious footsteps, rappings, moans, smells, cold drafts of air, loud crashing noises, and sightings of apparitions real or imagined? Certainly, as skeptics point out, a great many — in fact, most — of such manifestations can be explained by rational means. Nevertheless, there is a certain percentage of cases that remain in explicable.

Examples of these rare exceptions are included in this book. Again, I have no doubt of the honest and sincerity of those people who were good enough to share their stories with me. I believe that they believe — with the lone exception which is so noted in the text.

But as I have repeatedly said, my task is not to make converts to the believability of ghosts. It is merely to entertain; to pass along the fascinating accounts I have heard. So whatever your persuasion is or isn't, I hope you will find the following accounts as interesting and entertaining as I did.

Enjoy!

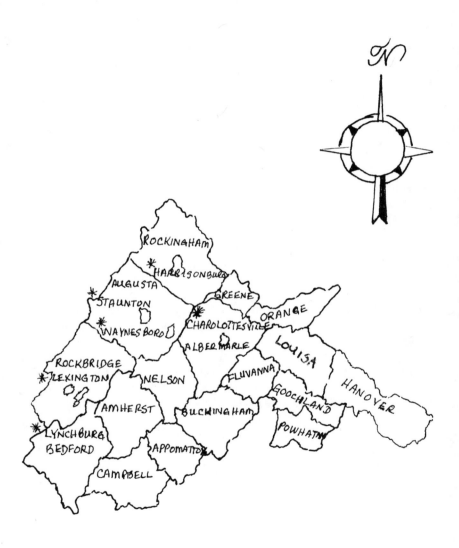

CENTRAL VIRGINIA

The Insolent Hostess
of Castle Hill

If there is any place by man's creation which approaches the great secret of nature, like the untouched woods or the ocean's floor, which calls forth our solemn admiration — that place is Castle Hill. Let us leave the shimmering fields 'neath an atmosphere which has created poets and philosophers."

— Quote from Historic Virginia Magazine

A funny thing happened to British Colonel Banastre Tarleton at historic Castle Hill in Charlottesville during the early morning hours of June 4, 1781. He and his troops got waylaid, in a friendly sort of way, by genial host Dr. Thomas Walker. And had not the good doctor detained the colonel and his men for as long as he did, the course of U.S. history may have been inexorably altered, and some have even surmised that America might have remained under English rule for years, perhaps decades or generations longer than it did!

More than 200 years after this curious yet crucial episode occurred, it almost mystically remains little more than an obscure historical footnote. Equally perplexing is the fact that the hero of this underplayed drama — Jack Jouett — likely would stump the panel on Jeopardy. Yet in terms of the importance of his contributions to the liberation of his nation, Jouett, experts will tell you, should rank as high on the scale, if not higher, than Paul Revere!

All Jouett did, through nearly superhuman effort, plus a welcome and necessary helping hand from Dr. Walker, was save the fledgling country's key legislators, including Thomas Jefferson himself, from virtually certain capture by Tarleton's forces. The ramifications of such an act are staggering to imagine. It would have been like the Union Army ensnaring generals Robert E. Lee and Stonewall Jackson together in the first months of the Civil War.

Here's how the story unfolded: On the evening of June 3, 1781, Jouett, a happy-go-lucky giant of a man at six foot four, and a captain in the Virginia militia, happened to be supping at the Cuckoo Tavern in Louisa County. He saw a large group of British cavalrymen outside, moving through the area. In fact, it was Colonel Tarleton, admiringly called by his contemporaries, "The Hunting Leopard." He had a force of 180 dragoons and 70 mounted infantrymen.

The fast-thinking Jouett quickly analyzed the seriousness of the moment. General Cornwallis had launched a spirited attack across Virginia, and as a precautionary measure, Jefferson, then Governor of Virginia, and about 40 key members of the legislature had "strategically retreated" from the colonial capitol in Richmond to the more remote Monticello. Jouett correctly surmised that Tarleton was sweeping stealthily toward Charlottesville in a surprise move to capture the Virginians. In addition to Jefferson, Patrick Henry, Richard Henry lee, Thomas Nelson, Benjamin Harrison, and many other noteworthy leaders were among the intended prey.

At about 10 p.m., after the troops had passed by, Jouett slipped onto his steed and headed due west to warn his fellow countrymen. As Tarleton took the main road, the redoubtable captain, aided by a full moon, struck out along an old Indian trial which had not been used for years. It was rough and dangerous ride through forests, thick patches of thistles and hanging wild grapevines. Jouett was to carry facial scars caused by the boughs of trees for the rest of his life. Nevertheless, he rode so hard for about 40 miles, that his horse gave out near Castle Hill. He told Dr. Walker of the situation and was given a fresh mount in the pre-dawn blackness. He continued on without rest.

A short time later, near daybreak, Tarleton and his men arrived at Castle Hill, stopped to rest, and demanded food. Dr. Walker and his wife obliged them. First, allegedly, they plied the officers with rounds of well spiked mint juleps, all the while telling the kitchen help to delay breakfast preparations as long as possible. The ploy worked. In fact, in a Historic Virginia Magazine article some years ago the writer reported that Tarleton "became quite irate at the delay in serving the meal, and stalked into the kitchen demanding the cause, whereupon the worth functionary, the colored cook, said 'De soldiers dun eat up two breakfuses as fast as I kin cook 'em.'" Tarleton then "ordered the men to be flogged, being first tied to a cherry tree, the site of which is still shown. They were most unmercifully whipped, their loud cries resounding over the place." By the time the colonel was able to remount his troops, Jouett has reached Monticello, and Jefferson and most of the legislators were able to escape.

It was a brilliant and heroic maneuver that helped shorten the war and secure the independence of the colonies. Yet, interestingly, it was, in the estimation of many historians, an event that has never been given due credit. For example, says eminent author Virginius Dabney, "It was a ride that overshadows Paul Revere's much more famous but far less difficult feat." Adds noted biographer Ellie Marcus Marx, in her book, "Virginia and the Virginians," published in 1930: "Had it not been for Jack Jouett's brave and timely ride, there would have been no Jefferson to help bring peace, happiness, and success to the American people."

Thus, stately Castle Hill not only figured prominently in a fascinating vignette of our heritage, but it also, through the centuries, has been host to a series of psychic manifestations. Strangely, they involve neither Jouett, Tarleton, or Dr. Walker. Rather, they center around the fussy and selective spirit of a woman who probably was an early resident in the mansion, and has "stayed around" to see that no further unwelcome intruders over indulge in the house's longtime reputation for outstanding hospitality.

The earliest portion of this two-part house was built by Dr. Walker in 1764 in the colonial Virginia frame tradition. It should be said here that Walker himself is a much under publicized contributor to the growth and success of the colony. John Hammond Moore, in his impressive history of the area, "Albemarle . . Jefferson's County," published in 1976, wrote: "Although 18th century Albemarle was the home of many distinguished citizens, one man, more than any other, left an indelible imprint upon the county's early history. For over half a century, whether tending to the sick, exploring the far slopes of the Appalachians and beyond, establishing the town of Charlottesville, speaking up for the welfare of the Piedmont in the House of Burgesses, supplying the Virginians fighting with Braddock, negotiating with Indian chiefs, or pursuing his special interests in scientific agriculture, religion, and commerce, Thomas Walker was a force to be reckoned with. From the moment he appeared in western Goochland County in the early 1740s until his death in 1794, just four months short of his 80th birthday, Walker was personally involved in every step which transformed the region he came to love from frontier settlement to established community."

Thus it should be no surprise to learn that some of the intellectual giants of that era were close friends of Walker, and often were guests at Castle Hill. It is recorded, for example, that Jefferson played his fiddle there on occasion, and that the youthful James Madison danced to the lively music. The original house was reportedly destroyed by Indians. The old porch in the rear was laid with large square stones that once were used for the walls of the structure.

The brick addition was erected in 1823-24 for then-owner William Cabell Rives, himself a U.S. Senator and Confederate congressman. It was, says the Virginia Landmarks Register, "an example of Jeffersonian classicism by the master builder John M. Perry." The brick was imported from England, with Tuscan Doric columns of white stucco running all across the front. The small panes of glass and brass door locks came from London.

In time, Castle Hill descended to Rives' granddaughter, Amelie, a distinguished novelist of her time. A remarkable woman in her own right, she began writing fiction and poetry as a pre and early teen, but was discouraged by a grandmother who took away her papers and pencils. Undaunted, she began writing her verses on the wide hems of her white starched petticoats. When her novel, "the Quick and the Dead," was published, in the late 1880s, she was but 25 years old and became instantly famous.

Photographs and sketches of Amelie lend physical proof to the general acknowledgement that she was one of the great beauties of the day, and that she carried this beauty throughout her life into old age. Born to the "social graces," she first married John Armstrong Chaloner, a man described as being the most eccentric in Albemarle County's history. While the marriage lasted only a short while, Chaloner was such a fanciful character, with a deep abiding interest in the occult, that it is worthwhile to briefly mention a few highlights of his life. On a trip to New York, he was somehow committed to an insane asylum. Several years later he escaped and returned to the Charlottesville area, where he was declared legally sane.

In March 1909, Chaloner shot and killed a drunken neighbor named John Gillard. Incredibly, when the police arrived, they found Chaloner, in his leather pajamas, eating his customary breakfast of duck and vanilla ice cream. He told the officers he had spent the night with Gillard's body "to test his nerve." Apparently, it was ruled self-defense, and later Chaloner went on the lecture circuit to talk about this bizarre affair. He also lectured on hell, lunacy reform laws, and on buzzards which, he feared, were facing extinction.

Irascible and unpredictable, Chaloner, according to historian/author John Hammond Moore, used his cane to smash windows of autos that came too close to him as he strolled city streets. He also reportedly once held a University of Virginia professor prisoner in his mansion, Merrie Mills, while he impersonated great figures of history. For all his eccentricities, however, he was, too, a generous man who gave a considerable portion of his sizeable fortune to the needy.

Divorced early from Chaloner, Amelie Rives next married Prince Pierre Troubetzkoy, a Russian painter of international repute. During their long tenure at Castle Hill it became a showcase for the Charlottesville gentry, complete with a magnificent garden shaped like an hour glass, and a fairway-sized front lawn lined by immense boxwoods.

In describing a first visit to Castle Hill in Historic Virginia Magazine some years ago, the writer seemed awed when he or she wrote: "On entering the portals of an extended lawn, which stretches for several hundred yards from the house, which even yet can scarcely be seen amidst the dense foliage, one is lifted in a transport of delight while circling through a maze of lofty oaks, developing ferns and fragrant evergreens.

"On every side Nature and Art seem to meet and kiss each other. On the one hand a tangled undergrowth of original forest, while on the other a long stretch of velvet green . . . that waft the perfumed air and cooling breeze in joyous welcome towards the visitor, who feels as if approaching the enchanted haven of peaceful rest, such as this beautiful home really possesses. . . . It is not until entering the wide hall and looking to the rear that one is struck with the beauty of its luxurious space, which the mansion presents in truly castellated style.

"Here true beauty and grace were wont to be displayed; here the poetry of song with the charm of social intercourse were heard; here every tree and shrub are linked with hallowed associations, where 'neath waving boughs and winding walks the noble countenances and handsome forms of presidents, statesmen, generals, authors, scientists, and divines have been seen; all make this historic old spot a real mecca, where the lover of true genius and noble worth can worship."

It was also during these years, including the early decades of the 20th century, that the hauntings first surfaced.

The manifestations took many forms. Guests reported to the Troubetzkoys that they heard footsteps ascending and descending the stairs late at night. Or they heard heavy pieces of furniture being moved around during the post-midnight hours. Some said they heard voices, but in leaving their bedrooms to check on the nocturnal conversationalists, found nothing. A number of visitors, plus the prince himself, told of smelling the distinct scent of roses, particularly on the stairways. Mrs. Troubetzkoy did not wear such perfume. Shaken servants came to the princess on several different occasions to tell her they had seen an apparition of her grandfather.

A former housekeeper at Castle Hill, identified in a 1982 article in Holiday Magazine as a "Mrs. Brown," said she was standing at the entrance to the study one day when "something grabbed my keys." She turned around, but no one was there. She lived in a cottage on the estate and said also there were times when "something" would grab her ankle if she slept on the bed without covers. She was asked if she thought these incidents were caused by a ghost. "I don't know how else you'd explain them," she replied. In more recent years, according to a 1985 article in the Charlottesville Daily Progress, overnight visitors have heard the "sounds of a lively party going on downstairs. They heard doors opening and shutting, chairs being pushed back against the drawing room walls, glasses clinking and music playing." No source for the apparent merry making was ever discovered.

While such phenomena was spread throughout the house, there was one particularly persistent spirit who seemed to confine her lively appearances to a certain room in the back of the house on the ground floor. It was known as the pink bedroom. Her exact identification has never been fully determined, although Mrs. Troubetzkoy, taking into account the descriptions given her by quite a few of her overnight guests, once said she believed the ghost to be her aunt, Amelie Louis Sigourney, who drowned with her husband and three children when their ship sank on their way to France in 1870. Those who caught glimpses of her said she was "not very old, rather pretty, and at times playful." Other contended she was downright frightful.

One who encountered her was writer Julian Green, who didn't believe in such things as spirits. However, after spending a night in the pink bedroom, he abruptly left Castle Hill early the next morning with scarcely a word of explanation to his hosts. Another who experienced a meeting with the strange lady was a gentleman from the University of Virginia who was to spend a Saturday and Sunday night in the house. When he appeared Sunday morning, though, he was pale and obviously uncomfortable. Without saying why, he, too, left in a rush.

It wasn't until a month later that the Troubetzkoys found out the reason for his hasty departure. A friend told the princess that the gentleman said he had been awakened in the middle of the night by a "charming looking woman dressed in the fashion of long ago, and carrying a tiny fan." He was, understandably, unnerved at the sight. The woman then told him, over and over, "You must please go. You must go away. You must not stay here."

The warning was more than enough. The gentleman said he would never again stay in that house. Later, when asked about specifics of the incident, he would mumble incoherently, wave his arms anxiously, and refuse steadfastly to discuss it further. Nor were these two the only ones to share the inhospitality of the apparitional hostess. At least three other people, including one woman, declared they not only were asked to leave the premises, they were, in their words, literally "pushed out of the house" by a sensation "not wanting them."

Yet, apparently, this ghost was selective in who she chose to drive out. Many visitors slept peacefully in the pink bedroom without a disturbance. The legend is that this room once belonged to the lady ghost and she, and only she, determines who may occupy it in peace. All others are given explicit psychic messages which they have unfailingly obeyed.

One must admit, it is a novel way to get rid of guests who have overstayed their welcome.

(Late in 1991, the Charlottesville Observer reported that Castle

Hill had been sold to the chairman of Columbia Pictures Television, Gary Lieverthal, who said he and his family planned to make it their home. He bought the house and 1,177 acres for $5.5 million, believed to be the second highest price ever paid for an estate in Albemarle County. The record occurred in 1988 when billionaire John Kluge paid $8.5 million for Morven.)

C H A P T E R   2

The Merry Spirits of Michie Tavern

s there a party still going on in the wee hours of the night at historic Michie Tavern on the outskirts of Charlottesville? There are some, including psychic experts and off-the-street tourists alike, who have sworn they have heard the raucous sounds of unbridled gaiety in and around the third floor ballroom of the tavern. And there is no denying that this room was the scene of many wing-dinging bashes during the days of our forefathers, more than 200 years ago.

But there seems to be a split in the opinion of the official hostesses at the site. Some today say such tales are likely figments of over active imaginations which have been embellished in the telling and retelling over the years. They contend the party ended centuries ago and there are no ghostly revelers in the old tavern today. Some of their fellow workers disagree strongly. "I'm sure there's a ghost here," said one recently. I personally haven't seen it, and it's always in the ballroom." "Is there a ghost on the third floor," another hostess repeated the question asked her. "Oh, yes. I haven't experienced it, but enough people have told me about it, so there must be something to it. They say they hear the noises of a party going on, things like that."

One lady even offered that there might be two spirits in the tavern area — one in the ballroom and quite another in the old general store and grist mill down the hill from the tavern proper. A subsequent inquiry to a cashier-hostess there drew a positive response. "Yes, there definitely is *something* here. 'He' opens cupboard doors at times, and we hear him walking around upstairs when all the tourists have gone for the day. We think he just wants to let us know

'he's' around."

So there remains some debate as to whether or not supernatural manifestations occur at Michie. Perhaps the spectral merry making may be heard only by the psychically sensitive which could well account for the difference in opinions. Either way, however, Michie (pronounced Mickey) Tavern is a splendid and colorful edifice that was, for eons, a favored stopover in stage coach days, and currently carries on that tradition of hospitality. At an adjacent, 200-year-old slave house called "The Ordinary," present-day visitors can be treated to typical dishes of the colonial period, including Southern fried chicken, blackeye peas, stewed tomatoes, cole slaw, potato salad, green bean salad, Tavern beets, homemade biscuits, cornbread and homemade apple cobbler. Local Virginia wines are available to "slake one's thirst."

The building itself was opened as a tavern in 1784 after Scotsman John Michie had purchased the land in 1746 from Patrick Henry's father. It was opened, the senior Michie said, to accommodate the many travelers seeking food and shelter at his home. Its original location was on Old Buck Mountain Road in the Earlysville area, about 17 miles from Charlottesville. Just what statesmen-celebrities frequented the place is a matter of conjecture. Actually, confusion might be a better word.

According to the accounts of many writers, including some area brochures, the Tavern was the one-time haunt of such giants of history as Jefferson, Madison, Monroe and Andrew Jackson. But in his fine history, "Albemarle: Jefferson's County," author John Hammond Moore indicates the only notable former guest cited by the Charlottesville Progress was "Lafayette, who, it was said once was put up there by Jefferson so he could enjoy a few days of hunting." Whatever, in 1927, the Inn was dismantled piece by piece and moved to its present location, near the city, on Route 53, close to both Monticello and Ash Lawn.

While it may be questionable as to who frequented Michie in the late 18th and early 19th centuries, it is nevertheless generally agreed that it has been beautifully restored and maintained in the traditions of that colorful era. The tavern contains a large and fine collection of pre-revolutionary furniture and artifacts, including many of those from the original Michie owners. William Michie's rifle, for instance, hangs over the mantel in the Keeping Hall.

It also is interesting to peruse a copy of the old tavern rules which were dispensed with stern authority in the 18th century. One specified, for example, that no more than five men could sleep in a bed at night. When one tours the tavern and sees the size of the beds, which are smaller than current double beds, one wonders how five people could even cram into such tight space, much less sleep. Boots in bed were forbidden, thankfully. The price was right. Lodging was cheaper than the evening meal; four pence a night for bed and six pence for supper. There was some discrimination, though. Organ grinders were relegated to sleep in the washhouse, and no razor grinders or tinkers were taken in!

The tavern has three floors and a large number of rooms. One of the most interesting — and the one many people say is haunted — is the ballroom on the third floor. It has a long-held reputation of harboring a cluster of ghosts. But they are friendly, high-spirited ones. It is in the ballroom that psychics and others psychically sensitive have said that they have heard the sounds of partying, and felt the presence of a group of men and women thoroughly enjoying themselves. They have heard and sensed this, but no one has seen any of the people participating in the fun making. The most common manifestations reported have included the distant sound of laughter, of gay music, and the tinkling of glasses.

Others have said and written that they felt some sort of confrontation, a kind of embarrassment, took place here. It also has been written that the waltz, introduced from Europe, was danced here in the ballroom for the first time in America. Tieing in with this, there is a legend that during the first waltz, a Charlottesville belle, a young girl, danced with a dashing Frenchman and he had held her closely. This had never been seen before, and caused considerable social shock waves through the town's gentry. It has been speculated that this was the alleged source of embarrassment that has been sensed there. As for the partying, well, there were many gala occasions in the ballroom two centuries ago.

Perhaps some of the participants enjoyed themselves so much, they decided to linger on and share their happiness with visitors from other eras. Whether one can "tune in" on such festivities today probably is doubtful, but then again, Michie is now, as it has been since 1784, a hospitable retreat from which the dust of the road can be pleasantly washed away.

Ballroom at Michie Tavern

CHAPTER 3

Tragedy at Tallwood

ne of the great families of Albemarle County was founded in the Green Mountain area by John Coles, an Irish immigrant who came to the Virginia colony probably sometime in the late 1730s. He prospered as a merchant in Richmond, moved west with the pioneers, bought 3,000 acres in the southern part of the county, and built a frame hunting lodge on the slopes of the mountain sometime in the mid-1740s. He called this modest house Enniscorthy after his Irish ancestral home.

Ensuing descendants of John Coles also did well and built some distinguished manor homes in the area, including Enniscorthy II and Enniscorthy III, Tallwood, Estouteville, Redlands, and others. At least two of them — Tallwood and Enniscorthy — have fascinating stories of psychic phenomena associated with them.

Tallwood, renowned for its English Yew trees, which lend sort of a ghostly atmosphere to the plantation, was originally part of the Enniscorthy estate. The original nucleus of the present house was built sometime in the middle of the 18th century. Tucker Coles inherited the property early in the 19th century and enlarged the mansion to its present general shape and size between 1805 and 1810. The broad, rambling home has 12 rooms. Tucker's wife, Helen, laid out a magnificent garden next to the yews, with superb specimens of crepe myrtle, lilac, mock orange and other shrubs.

The happening at Tallwood is told by Elizabeth Langhorne, a family descendent who has carried on the long Coles tradition of distinguished community service. She has been lecturer at the University of Virginia School of Continuing Education and at Piedmont Community College, and also a guest curator at the University of Virginia Museum of Art. She has authored several books, including "Monticello: A Family Story;" "The Golden Age of Albemarle: A Portrait Show;" and "A Virginia Family and Its

Plantation Houses."

"Here we are," she says, looking up the date of the particular incident which has fostered the manifestations which have periodically reoccurred in the more than 100 years since. "It was November 7, 1879. That was the date when the so-called 'accident' happened." Mrs. Langhorne is talking about her aunt, Selina, who lived at Tallwood at the time with her older brother, Peyton S. Coles, Jr.

"There were 12 children in their family, and the two oldest, Peyton and Selina had gone to live in the house which they had inherited from their aunt," Mrs. Langhorne says. "I am 82 now, but I never knew her, of course. My father wasn't married until he was in his middle age. But this was the story he used to tell me. It's been in the family a long time.

"Shortly after they began living there, the maid was starting to clean Peyton's room one day, when she came out and told Selina that she was afraid to continue because there was a gun on the shaving stand, and she had a fear of such weapons. Selina, who had no such fear, said not to worry, she would go in and remove the gun.

"The next thing anyone knew, after a few minutes, there was a shot from Peyton's bedroom, and the maid ran in to find her mistress on the floor, dead from a gunshot wound. I think everyone more or less assumed it had been an accident. It seems to me very unlikely

that this is how it happened. Selina was familiar with guns, so it just seems impossible to me that it could have been an accident. But why she might have shot herself, I don't have any real idea.

"Anyway," Mrs. Langhorne continues, "from that time on it was said that every November 7th a certain window in the room would open by itself and a fresh breeze would blow in. That is what my father told me." It is also said that some people refused to go into the room on that date.

The other phenomenon took place at Enniscorthy III. the predecessor house, Enniscorthy II, had been built in 1784, and, as one author phrased it, "became the gathering place for such noted Virginians as Jefferson, Madison, Monroe and Patrick Henry." It was at this site that Jefferson had sent his wife and daughters for safety when Colonel Tarleton was approaching Monticello.

Surrounded by fields, mills, slave cabins, and acres of great trees, shrubs and plants, Enniscorthy II, a "great rambling house" was the long established home for Coles family for more than 50 years. Mrs. Langhorne writes that at the time, "one did not doubt that it would last forever." Then, on a cold wintry day, the last Monday of December 1839, a strong gale was blowing from the northwest. As Mrs. Langhorne described it, "From some hearth or chimney a shower of sparks had risen; flames had caught and gone roaring with the wind against the gable end of the house. Once started, no effort availed, the whole house went. Only the portraits and some furniture were saved."

Also devoured by the intense fire, were every last shrub and plant which had so picturesquely ringed the house, including a prized rose bush. Nothing was left. Everything had been burned to the bare ground.

From these ashen ruins, Enniscorthy III, a two story brick house arose in 1850, built by Isaac Coles' widow, Juliana Stricker Coles. It stands proud today.

Mrs. Langhorne says that soon after the new home was erected, a photograph was taken of it. In the picture the prized rosebush that burned in 1839 appears! "I can't explain it," she says. "But I have seen the photograph. It is there. There's no mistaking it."

C H A P T E R   4

Long and Lonely Vigil at Castalia

If there ever was any doubt that Charlottesville and the surrounding area did not have more than its share of ghostly hauntings, it surely must have been dispelled, once and for all, by the detailed investigatory work and lengthy writings of Hans Holzer. Holzer is a world-renowned parapsychologist, and is, quite possibly, the best known authority on ghosts in the United States. In fact, he considers Charlottesville to be one of the most haunted cities, for its size, in the country. He has visited several times and he has written extensively about area psychic phenomena. He has covered such historic sites as Monticello, Ash Lawn, Castle Hill, and many others. And when he delves into a haunting, he does it first-class. In Charlottesville, for example, during his trips there in the 1960s and 1970s, he was escorted by two of Albemarle County's most respected historians — Virginia Cloud and Horace Burr. He also has been accompanied by a psychic friend of his, Ingrid Beckman, who had the ability to walk into an old house and sense activities that took place there 200 or more years ago.

Such was the case when Holzer, about 20 years ago, looked into, and confirmed, the time-honored traditions of supernatural occurrences at Castalia, a venerable three-story manor home built in 1850 that stands in "lonely majesty" in the countryside a few miles from the center of town. A sweeping veranda wraps around most of the house, setting off the portico, which is flanked by towering red brick chimneys. Holzer and his entourage were impressed with Castalia's interior, which he said "without a single intrusion of modernism or so-called improvements . . . was a joy to the eye." He was impressed by the thick carpets, heavy drapes, beautifully carved staircases, and multiple rooms, furnished with early 19th century pieces.

There are two ghostly legends associated with Castalia — one outside, and one inside. A number of area old-timers have told of seeing a spectral rider on horseback ahead of them as they approached the house on the road that connects into another haunted mansion, Castle Hill. The reports of this particular phenomenon vary little in the recounting: the pale rider "leads" visitors to the house as if he were assigned as an escort. Then he vanishes. No one at home ever sees him, no one knows who he is or where he goes. It could be speculated, however, that he is somehow connected with the spirit of a woman who made her sad presence known inside the walls of Castalia for decades.

She, too, has been witnessed or "felt" by several people over the years. Sightings of this wraith-like figure were made from the 1920's to the 1940's by members of the Boocock family, which owned the home at the time. Mrs. Lila Boocock, for instance, was visiting her relatives at the house in 1926 when one night she said she was awakened by "a little woman with dark brown hair, pulled back, wearing a shawl and a striped taffeta dress." She appeared to be shuffling through some legal-looking papers. Mrs. Boocock sat bolt upright in bed and said she distinctly heard a sound which reminded her of "crisp onions being cut" as the woman riffled through the papers. The apparition then walked straight to the edge of the bed, smiled faintly, and appeared to want to say something. The next instant she disappeared.

Another relative who experienced a different manifestation was Elizabeth Boocock. She woke up one morning in 1929 at five a.m. to the rhythmic patter of footsteps, which she described as sounding like "one-two-three-stop." She thought at first that her husband, who had been ill, might have gotten up and was pacing around upstairs. But she found him asleep in his bed. In the next few days she heard the same footstep pattern repeated, always at five in the morning. When she inquired about it, her in-laws told her not to be concerned, that it was probably their resident ghost.

A third accounting came from one of the Boocock daughters, Gwendolyn Goss. It occurred in 1943 when she and a friend of hers were staying overnight in what is called the Chintz room. She remembers it was a cold night and there was a fire in the fireplace. The two young women put their clothes over a chair near the fire and went to bed. In the middle of the night Gwendolyn heard some noise and assumed her friend had gotten up. Her friend heard the same noise and made the same assumption. The both got up and turned on the lights. To their astonishment, they found their clothes scattered on the floor, and the chair "turned toward the fireplace with an open book on it." Gwendolyn said that neither one of them had put the book there, and she also recalled that the room had turned icy cold, a strong indication that they had had a visitation from someone in the spirit world. She added that she later heard the same sounding footsteps that her mother had.

On another occasion, Gwen came home from school for a weekend and was alone in the house on a Friday night when her parents went out to a dinner party. That is, she was alone except for her dog, Flossie, a cocker spaniel. By 9 p.m., Gwen called her parents, terrified, and asked them to come home immediately. She had heard a loud noise upstairs. This was not footsteps or stairs creaking or anything like that. It was a loud noise! She told Flossie to "sic em," and the obedient dog went charging up the stairs, but quickly came back down the stairs obviously badly frightened and totally out of character for the normally feisty dog. Her parents searched the house when they returned, but nothing was found out of order.

Gwen also once reported hearing a "terrible noise" in one of the newer addition rooms at Castalia. She said it sounded like "someone had grabbed a runner from a table full of pictures and objects. I came bolting down the stairs, but everything was in place." There was, too, a brief chance meeting of the ghost and one of the maids. The maid was on her way to breakfast when, as she put it, she turned around and saw "this little old woman wearing a white cap." The maid didn't think much about the incident until she asked a family member who the company was. When she was told there were no guests in residence her face turned as white as the apparition's cap.

There were also unexplained "crashes" in both the Chintz and Lavender rooms, sounding like someone had swept all the glassware off the tops of bureaus. But each time nothing was found amiss in the rooms. At other times, lights were mysteriously turned on in certain rooms with no rational explanation ever advanced.

Yet another strange incident happened once when the Boocock family closed up the house for a period in the 1930s while they vacationed in Europe. Castalia was locked up tighter than a drum, not only from the outside, but each individual room also was sealed. As one member of the family put it, "a mouse couldn't have gotten in." Prior to their homecoming, the Boococks wired their maid and farm manager to prepare the house for their return. When the servants unlocked the so-called Lavender room, they found the bedspread and a bureau scarf piled in a heap on the floor, and all the silver strewn around, as if "someone had gone through it in a fit of temper." A subsequent search revealed no one else in the house.

The question piqued the Boococks for years. Who was this ethereal woman and why was she there? Was she searching for something? The Holzer visit provided some possible answers. His psychic friend, Ingrid, carefully probed each room in the house and seemingly peered through time, gaining some insightful impressions. She envisioned an "older woman" on an all night vigil, waiting for her man to return to Castalia. She said the woman was agitated and deeply worried that "he" would never return. That might explain the recurrence of the footsteps. The woman could have been pacing the floor. Ingrid believed that whoever it was she was waiting for had been killed, probably in battle. The psychic further sensed that the old woman eventually grew ill, and moved her vigil from the Chintz room to the Lavender room, where she died. But her spirit never left the house. She remained over the centuries in hopes of seeing her man come home. Could the man have been the phantom rider so many had seen approach the house from the road leading in? Possibly, but this was not determined.

Ingrid said the ghost was stubborn and would not readily accept the fact that both she and the man had died. At this point, in contact with the spirit, the psychic tried to explain the situation, but it was difficult for "her" to understand. Ingrid described the apparition the same as the Boococks had, saying she was wearing "a white shawl bordered with fringes." Holzer, who wrote about the incident in his book, "Great American Ghost Stories," said that Ingrid, finally, was able to persuade her that she didn't have to wait any longer. From that time on, her appearances ceased, her long suffering at last ended.

But the question remained. Who was she? Some theories were offered. It could have been a woman whose husband had been killed in Revolutionary War fighting that took place in the Charlottesville area. Or it could have been one of the descendants of Dr. Thomas Walker, the master of Castle Hill. One of his grandsons was named Lewis and he is said to have lived at Castalia in the mid-1800s and was allegedly killed in a hunting accident. It could have been his widow who waited so long for him to return. She was known to have had straight, pulled back hair and she wore a shawl and a striped taffeta dress, which matched the apparitional vision Lila Boocock saw.

Whoever she was, Ingrid Beckman apparently was able to finally put her troubled mind at ease and free her spirit to perhaps reunite with her man in another world.

CHAPTER 5

A Trilogy of
Feminine Mystique

or some unexplained reason, the great majority of apparitional figures, especially those
seen in older houses, seem to be women. Some appear as shadowy
or gauzy, wraith-like figures, semi-transparent. Others are fully
clothed, often in grayish garb which dates to earlier eras. Experts
have offered few, if any theories as to why this is. Possibly it is
because the women of colonial and ante-bellum times were in their
houses a lot more than their men. They were the ones who tended
sick and sometimes dying children and who looked after the upkeep
of their homes.

Whatever the reason, following are three separate accounts of
ghostly females who returned to three houses in and around
Charlottesville in days gone by.

* * * * *

VISIONS AT SUNNY BANK

Sunny Bank is a venerable Albemarle County house in the South
Garden vicinity, located about 18 miles out of Charlottesville. It was
built in 1797, and according to the Virginia Landmarks Register, is
"an imposing if somewhat provincial version of the Palladian tripar-
tite scheme introduced to the region with the first form of
Monticello." It stands upon an "eminence" from which there are
commanding panoramic views, and it is flanked by several original
outbuildings and a formal garden. Fresh springs wind their way
through the meadows at the foot of the hill. Its first owner was

Andrew Hart, son of a Scottish clergyman, who became a prominent local planter and merchant. The house has remained in the family for nearly 200 years.

According to legends, as reported by Margaret DuPont Lee in her book, "Virginia Ghosts," published in 1930, and as told by members of the Hart family and others, there are two ghosts of young women at Sunny Bank who died in the house. And, in the early part of the 20th century, they apparently made their presence known through a variety of psychic manifestations which were witnessed by several surviving Harts. The phenomena included: mysterious footsteps on the stairway which could not be accounted for; the clear sound of water being poured into a basin by unseen hands; the rocking of empty chairs in vacant rooms; and the repeated clatter of a horse and buggy being driven up to the front door, though no visitors were ever sighted.

One of the spectral ladies apparently needed a new outfit at one time in the 1920s, for when a family member reached into her wardrobe one afternoon and selected a pretty striped silk dress to wear — one that she hadn't worn in some time — she found that it had been cut and altered into a size so petite she couldn't get into it. Further, said Mrs. Andrew de Jarnette Hart, "the passementerie (a fancy edging or trimming) had been sewn on exquisitely; the daintiest of stitches. No one here did it and it has ever been a mystery."

Mrs. Hart also said she had awakened one morning earlier in the century and saw the profile of a young woman dressed in white "of a lovely ethereal appearance," sitting on the edge of her bed. In seconds, the vision vanished. Mrs. Hart believed this to be the spirit of her husband's sister, Betty Dew, who died in that room. On another occasion, a guest, Anne Byrd, saw a woman standing before the bureau combing what she described as "the most resplendent hair." It was in that room that another member of the family, Constance Cazenove, had died. She was known for her beautiful long tresses.

It is probable, too, that there is a third visitor from another world at Sunny Bank. There was, decades ago, an old lady staying at the house who "persisted in roaming out of doors." For her protection, the Harts kept the front door tightly locked. They believe it is she who periodically shook the door violently when no one was nearby. A number of guests saw her dressed in black and wearing white stockings suggesting the fashions of a long ago period.

* * * * *

CATASTROPHE AT CARRSGROVE

The returning presence of another female ghost — this one with deep overtones of tragedy — has long haunted a historic Charlottesville house known as Carrsgrove. It was built of stone by David Reese in 1748, well before the city was established. A young James Monroe, the master of Ash Lawn and future President of the United States, visited here a number of times during the Revolutionary War. Monroe's brother, in fact, bought the house in 1797, and then sold it to James three years later when he was governor of Virginia. He lived at Carrsgrove for nine years.

Other famous names also have been associated with the house. A lavish party was thrown here in 1824 for the Marquis de Lafayette when he visited Charlottesville during his farewell tour of America. During the Civil War the golden-haired General George Armstrong Custer made the house his headquarters for a time. Horace Burr, a direct descendent of Aaron Burr, bought Carrsgrove in 1955, and it is he and his wife, Helen, who told of ethereal happenings. They mostly took the form of a woman sobbing. At other times, a sturdy chandelier shook for no apparent reason.

Helen Burr first noticed the strange happenings which curiously seemed to occur always at precisely 3:45 in the morning. After experiencing this several times, she woke her husband one day and he went with her to a spot near an inner wall where the gasping, moaning sound could be heard. He heard it, too. Intrigued, Burr, a noted historian and art authority, conducted extensive research to find the cause for the somber atmosphere that seemed to envelope the house on occasion. He found a plausible explanation. It seemed a young mother lived in the house once — the period has not been determined — and she was nursing a very sick child, a girl. The child was delirious for some time and unresponsive to either medical treatment, or the unrequited love of her mother. Over time, the woman sank into a state of depression, fearing that her daughter either would not recover, or if she did, she would be severely deformed.

It became too much for the mother to take. She took poison. Her mournful last gasps were heard by her father down the hall in the master bedroom, but she died before he could reach her. Ironically, the child recovered and grew up to be a "perfectly normal and beautiful young woman." Thus, Burr believed, it was the mother who returned to the house in spirit form, longing to be reunited.

A BROODING PRESENCE AT BREMO RECESS

The plantation has been called "the ultimate in enchantment and beauty and a home sufficiently large to make gracious living an art." The author of that half-century-old magazine article quotation was speaking of Bremo Recess, or Recess Bremo — it is referred to both ways; a splendid historic home on the James River in Fluvanna County. It is part of a complex of mansions including Upper Bremo and Lower Bremo all created by a Virginia planter, soldier and reformer of note, General John Hartwell Cocke. "Recess" was the first to be built, in 1803. It has been described as a "by no means large, but picturesque and quaint old brick dwelling," and it has said to have been patterned after the architecture of Bacon's Castle near Surry, one of the Commonwealth's oldest buildings.

It is, however, the gardens and grounds of Recess which have drawn admiration and praise over the years. Within ivy-covered stone walls, the Cockes and their successors tended a veritable Garden of Eden. It was best known for its sumptuous pear trees and a forest of fig trees. Apples, peaches and raspberries also grew in abundance, not to mention healthy vineyards of Scuppernong grapes. All of this — "a tribute to the handiwork of man and the bounteous powers of nature" — was colorfully decorated by seas and seas of forsythia, lilies and "old fashioned pinks."

The feminine mystique at this house was associated with a gentleman named Dr. Lewis Greene. In the year 1910, while he was a visitor there, the family went out to a party one evening, leaving him alone. The doors were locked. Dr. Greene decided to read. Before settling down with his book, however, he placed a bottle of wine, Scuppernong perhaps, and some crackers on the dining room table so the family members could refresh themselves when they returned.

In the midst of his reading, the doctor noticed a shadow pass over his book. He looked up and saw a woman standing before him wearing a bright green skirt. Shaken, he rubbed his eyes, got up and followed her into the dining room, but "there she was not."

When the family came home, before Dr. Greene could inform them of what had happened, they went into the dining room. The wine had disappeared, and the doctor stammered that he had put a bottle there for them earlier. "The ghost must have taken it," he exclaimed. As he said this "the face of one of those present blanched," and the family members steadfastly refused to discuss the matter.

The Mystery Hummer
of Monticello

What can be said about the grandeur, the magnificence of Monticello that has not already been said thousands of times over by the most gifted of writers during the past two centuries? One of the brochures on the racks at the Thomas Jefferson Visitor Center three miles southeast of Charlottesville just off Route 20 puts it well: "often described as one of our country's foremost architectural masterpieces . . . Monticello remains today as a testimony to its creator's ingenuity and breadth of interests. Located on a mountaintop in Albemarle County, the house commands a view of the rolling Virginia Countryside that Jefferson so dearly loved. It was here that he retreated from the pressures of public office. . ."

Even the usually conservative Virginia Landmarks Register effused over its description of the house: "There is no more admired or intriguing home in America than . . . Monticello. Reflecting the genius and versatility of its creator, the estate is a monument to the most scrupulous contemporary thought in the field of architecture, landscaping, agriculture, and domestic comforts. The house, fortuitously preserved with few significant changes, is filled with ingenious devices and mementos of a man who influenced much of the history of the nation and indeed the world."

Jefferson began his complex dwelling on the "Little Mountain" in 1770 and worked on it for over 40 years, altering and enlarging it as his taste developed. . . when an extensive revision was finished in 1809, it had become an amalgam of Roman, Palladian, and French architectural ideals, all rendered in native materials and scale to form a unique statement by one of history's great individuals.

But of all the literary efforts of 200 years, who could paint the scene with more heart-felt exquisiteness than The Man himself. In 1786, he penned: "And our own dear Monticello, where has nature spread so rich a mantle under the eye? Mountains, forests, rocks, rivers. With what majesty do we there ride above the storms! How sublime to look down into the workhouse of nature, to see her clouds, hail, snow, rain, thunder, all fabricated at our feet! And the glorious Sun, when rising as if out of a distant water, just gilding the tops of the mountains, and giving life to all nature!"

One young hostess did say that back in the 1920s when Monticello was first opened to public tours the guides were "older black men" whose only pay was tips from the tourists. "They figured the better the stories they told, the better their tips would be, and they came up with some good ones," she said. "They told of soldiers during the Civil War riding their horses in the house, and there were tales of beds rising up to the ceiling, but there never was any substantiation."

Surely, it would be this author's capstone if there were an epic ghost story to relate about Monticello; if Jefferson's imposing figure would occasionally reappear on the grounds or in the house, inspecting, tinkering, observing, enjoying again the splendors of his beloved estate. But such is not the case. Most of the historical interpreters politely say that they know of no Jeffersonian spirit, full of pluck and curiosity, roaming about. What a shame!

And yet, privately, there are a few references, here and there, to mysterious footsteps and other sounds; to certain "things" that admittedly are difficult to explain in television-age rationality. And there are even some who, through inexplicable personal experiences, have been persuaded that, indeed, perhaps there is an otherworldly presence here.

There are, in fact, some psychically-related vignettes to consider, for example. The spectral apparitions of Jefferson and his close friend, James Monroe, were sighted once 30 years ago by a man names Lawrence G. Hoes outside Monroe's law office in Fredericksburg. Hoes, a respected Virginian who almost single-handedly was responsible for the preservation of this historic building, swore he saw the two great men, dressed in colonial costume, having an animated debate outside the front door of the office. (This encounter is covered in its entirety in "The Ghosts of Fredericksburg.") When Hoes approached them, he said they vanished before his eyes, entering the building through the door. They didn't open the door and walk in. They walked *through* the door! Hoes rushed inside after the visions and demanded of the tour guide there to know where the two gentlemen had gone. They had seen nothing, and a thorough search of the premises found nothing. Psychic experts believe, for a few fleeting seconds, Hoes had entered into a historical "time warp."

There is, too, the curious fact that both John Adams, the second President of the United States, and Jefferson, the third President, at ages 90 and 83 respectively, died within hours of each other on the same day. And that day was July 4, 1826 — *50 years to the day* after the signing of the Declaration of Independence! Adams said on his death bed, "Jefferson still lives," not knowing that his fellow statesman had died a few hours earlier. Was this a rare coincidence, or was it psychically related?

There is one other anecdotal footnote to add to such a collection. There is a room, off the center room at Carters Grove plantation near Williamsburg, itself one of the classic and beautiful colonial mansions. It is called the "Refusal Room." Professional guides there will tell you that on separate occasions George Washington and Thomas Jefferson each was turned down by a young lady after they offered a proposal of marriage. In the dark hours of the night when the house is all still, someone, or something, enters and shreds the carnation pedals, strewing them all over the floor. Maids, cleaning people, guides and others, to this day, do not know who does this, but the strong impression is that one of the two jilted lovers, or possibly both, return to vent their disappointment.

Certainly, one could make a case for the justification of a Jefferson reappearance at Monticello, aside from his unquestioned love for the place. He could have been unhappy that his survivors, weighted in heavy debts, had to sell the plantation in 1831, five years after he died, to a druggist who tried, unsuccessfully, to grow silkworms on the farm. (Although it could be said, too, that Jefferson might have been pleased with such an experiment, since he was interested in just about everything!) Or he could have been upset when a subsequent owner, Uriah Phillips Levy or New York, tried to will the house to the Commonwealth of Virginia, only to have a nephew overturn the will. (The Thomas Jefferson Memorial Foundation eventually bought the property in 1923.)

The Man could have been displeased at all the unfavorable publicity that had swirled about him in recent years. Although generally unfounded and totally refuted by most historians, such gossip persists, contending that Jefferson had illicit liaisons with a slave or slaves at Monticello. It is alleged that he had a long standing tryst with Sally Hemings, and that they met often in a small dependent building on the grounds, and that Sally bore his children.

While much has been written about this in the past 20 years, including an account in Gore Vidal's best selling novel, "Burr," the slanderous story actually got its start nearly 200 years ago. The author was a political enemy of Jefferson's named James Thompson Callender. Furious when Jefferson, then President, did not appoint him to the position of postmaster of Richmond, Callender unleashed his attack, contending that Sally Hemings was Jefferson's concubine. Despite lacking a basis in fact, the tale spread like wildfire. In 1802, Callender placed the following ad in the Richmond Recorder: "Sally's business makes a prodigious noise here. You may save yourself the trouble of a moment's doubt in believing the story. But what will your pious countrymen upon the Connecticut say to such African amours? After this discovery I do not believe that, at the next election of 1804, Jefferson could obtain two votes on the Eastern side of the Susquehanna; and I think hardly four upon this side of it. He will, therefore, be laid aside . . . As for (James) Madison, he is a poor consumptive thing; five foot two or three inches high; deeply wrinkled, and nothing but skin and bone. He has not the constitution capable of supporting official fatigue." (Madison also would thus have cause to return to in the face of such despicable mud slinging.)

One well known writer on psychic phenomena said that there apparently had always been "a problem between Jefferson and his wife concerning other women. All of this did not contribute to Mrs. Jefferson's happiness." The author went on to ask, "Could it be that part of Thomas Jefferson still clings to this little cottage where he found much happiness?" Would such besmirching of his long-unassailable reputation not be sound reason for him to come back and clear the air, so to speak?

And then there is the long unpleasantness that clouded his final resting place, down the mountainside a ways, west of the house.

Gravesite of Thomas Jefferson

Jefferson himself had carefully designed his own tombstone, and left instructions that he was to be buried beside his brother-in-law and closest friend, Dabney Carr. The family cemetery was laid out over a choice acre of ground about half way up on the north side of the mountain. No one, not even the Sage of Monticello himself, could have imagined the terrible desecrations that were to follow his interment.

In 1879, his great grandson, Dr. Wilson Cary Nicholas Randolph, wrote in the Jeffersonian Gazette: ". . .When it was certain that no creditor would lose aught by Jefferson, his grandson erected a monument over his grave as was designed before his death by Jefferson . . .Twice has the marble slab over his wife and daughter been renewed, and once the granite obelisk over Jefferson's own grave. Now there is not a vestige of the slabs left, and the last obelisk chipped and battered by so called relic seekers, is a standing monument to American Vandalism . . "

It was bad enough that armies of tourists were boldly stalking off with chunks of tombstones, but then, from nowhere, came a movement to have Jefferson's body uplifted and taken north, to the Washington area. The northern press picked up on the idea and favored it strongly. Family descendants had to literally mount an attack to keep the body at rest at home. Finally, one newspaper, The New York Mercury, brought some sensibility to the bizarre situation. The paper said that, " Jefferson's bones had no business in such a place as Washington in 1882, . . to which the angels must pay few visits indeed. At Monticello, lifted near the sky, and situated amid sylvan glories, there is peace and purity. Mountain ozone is there, instead of the malaria of the Potomac flats, and the effusoria of political corruption. Let Jefferson's bones alone. They are in honest earth, in an honest atmosphere, and among honest citizens. . ."

With that, the ill-conceived movement subsided. But the vandals continued defacing the small cemetery for years afterward. Ordinary people with ghoulish bents squeezed through the iron bars surrounding the small cemetery and chipped with their hammers at anything they could find. Those who couldn't wriggle through the bars hired young boys to do their damage.

It really wasn't until well into the 20th century, when the Thomas Jefferson Memorial Foundation began restoring the buildings and grounds, and Monticello became a national shrine, that the vandalism ceased. Only then, as his great-granddaughter, Sarah Randolph, wrote, could "he sleep amid scenes of surpassing beauty and grandeur, on that lovely mountainside, surrounded by the graves of his children and grandchildren to the fifth generation....

The modesty of the spot is in striking contrast with the celebrity of its dead, and there are few in America of greater historical interest or more deserving of the nation's care."

Again, would not such actions stir the dead? Would it not be fitting for Jefferson to return to answer his caustic critics and to scold those who would disturb his grave site?

Or he might just return for the simple reason that, in life, he enjoyed so much happiness here.

Perhaps he does!

Some staff members at Monticello say that on occasion, after the mansion is closed for the day, they have heard the sound of a man humming a cheerful tune when there is no living mortal around.

Jefferson's overseer, Edmund Bacon, once wrote that Jefferson" ...was nearly always humming some tune or singing in a low tone to himself."

C H A P T E R 7

The Phantom Rocker at Ash Lawn

homas Jefferson had Monticello, his magnificent manor home atop a hill overlooking his beloved Charlottesville. And he certainly had enough interests to occupy his time — from farming to architecture to wine making to absorbing himself in his impressive library, and on and on. One thing The Man was lacking to a degree, however, in the semi-seclusion of his Albemarle retreat, was the spirited stimulation of conversations with his intellectual contemporaries.

In fact, Jefferson sought to develop "a society to our taste" in the vicinity of Monticello; a dream that eventually helped lead his friend and presidential successor, James Madison, to residence at Montpelier in Orange County. He also encouraged another close friend and long-time statesman associate, James Monroe, fifth President of the United States, to move to a site only two and a half miles from Monticello.

There, at a 535-acre tobacco farm first known as Highland, Jefferson sent his own gardeners to plant orchards even before Monroe moved in. The tract was on the east side of Carter's Mountain, a few miles southeast of the town of Charlottesville. Monroe and his wife, Elizabeth Kortright of New York, moved there in November 1799, and changed the name of the house from Highland to Ash Lawn. It was to be their home, off and on, except for the eight years Monroe lived in the White House, for the next 26 years.

By plantation and manor standards, it was not impressive. The original portion of the house, in fact, was called a "simple cottage." It was modest because the future president was in debt at the time of its construction. Still, he called it his "castle cabin," and he undoubtedly relished his long conversations and leisurely dinners over Madeira wine with his illustrious neighbor. The "cabin" eventually was enlarged in 1860 with the addition of a two-story porticoed section. More recently, the philanthropist Jay Winston Johns bequeathed Ash Lawn in 1974 to his alma mater, the College of William and Mary in Williamsburg, Virginia. It has been faithfully restored and today is open to the public as a museum commemorating Monroe's Albemarle County residency.

There is a specific ghostly phenomenon associated with the house, but guides and hostesses at the site are reluctant to discuss it. It involves an antique rocking chair in one of the small rooms. This chair allegedly rocks away all on its own, on occasion, with no one in it. Members of the Joseph Massey family, former owners, have reported seeing the chair in action a number of times, although there is some confusion as to just which members experienced the rocking.

Margaret DuPont Lee, in her 1930 classic book, "Virginia Ghosts," says it was Joseph Massey who told her about the incident. The parapsychology expert Hans Holzer, wrote in his 1991 book, "America's Haunted Houses," that it was a Mrs. J. Massey who saw the spectacle. Perhaps both did. The Massey family did own the home at one time. They said they had seen the chair rocking by itself, and either (or both of them) said their brother John also saw it. (They both must have had a brother named John.) Both said they had no qualms talking about it, and that it appeared as if someone were sitting in the chair at the time. The chair would continue to rock until one or the other of the Masseys touched it. Then it stopped.

Who is the mystery rocker? There was at least one mention, in an article written by reporter Mary Beth Donahue of the Charlottesville Daily Progress some years ago, of a "pretty girl" who draped her long hair over the back of the rocking chair to dry it by the fire. According to Donahue's source, the girl's hair "caught fire and she was burned to death." Allegedly, it is she who can be heard crying on cold nights, although the reporter did note that "more level-headed observers contend it is the resident peacocks making the crying noises."

Holzer conjectures that it might be a spirit so attached to his former home and refuge from the affairs of state that "he" still likes to sit in it, rock, and think things over. If it is indeed, Monroe, it is not the only known incident of psychic phenomena associated with him. He reportedly was seen in an animated discussion, possibly even an argument, with Thomas Jefferson in front of the Monroe law office

and museum in Fredericksburg in the 1960s by one of his distant descendants.

Throughout history there have been some famous presidential psychic encounters. George Washington, for example, allegedly had a vision one night in his camp headquarters in New Jersey in which he foresaw future wars America would be involved in, including the Civil War and World Wars I and II. One reported witness said the general was visibly shaken by the experience, although most Washington scholars doubt it ever happened. Abraham Lincoln was said to have dreamed of his impending assassination one night while visiting a Union fort in Virginia late in the Civil War.

Whether or not it was Monroe who rocked in the chair, Ash Lawn is well worth a side trip from Monticello, and the nearby historic Michie Tavern. There are summer music festivals, and at Christmas time, madrigals are sung and the home can be toured by candlelight. But alas, the puzzling mystery of the rocker likely will never be solved. On a recent visit to the house the chair mentioned by the Masseys was no where to be seen, and the hostess could offer no explanation as to where it had gone. Perhaps it rocks unseen somewhere in a dusty attic or in storage where the phantom rocker can contemplate the affairs of the world without being disturbed by curious tourists.

The Persnickety Spirit at Glenmore

he majority of haunted houses are said to be inhabited by the spirit or spirits of someone who had lived there in past years, often even centuries ago. If the ghost feels "comfortable" with the current owners of the home, its presence is seldom experienced, and even if they "reappear" it is usually in a friendly or benign manner. But if the former resident is unhappy, either with whom is presently living in "their house," or with what has been or is being done to the place in the form of renovations or modifications, the chances are greater that they will make their displeasure known in the form of some kind of manifestation.

Such apparently was the case with historic Glenmore in Albemarle County, a manor home which predates the Revolutionary War. This is a structure that has consistently been added to and altered over the past 200 years, and it appears some of the revamping pleased the spectral being and some didn't. The original building contained only one room, with a deep basement, all of which was constructed with massive stone walls packed with clay. Sometime in the late 1700s, a two-story frame addition was put on with two rooms on each floor and a porch was added. Several decades later another room was added to the second floor.

Between 1843 and 1856 many more modifications were made. Wings were placed on the east and west ends, the 75-foot front porch and an upstairs porch were built, and the staircase was moved from the front of the entrance way to the rear. A brick kitchen, with rooms for house servants, was built on the back lawn, and a law office and a smaller "mini replica" of the main house were put up in front.

It seems to have been these large-scale architectural changes which stirred the indignity of the resident spirit. "He" also was upset when a swimming pool was added more recently where an old vegetable garden once had been, not far from the family cemetery. At least that was what Mrs. L. Clay Camp thought when she was interviewed for a newspaper article in the 1970s. "My husband and I have never seen or heard him," she said, "but plenty of other people have. Actually, we're probably the only people who will spend the night alone in the house. More than once we've had people get up in the middle of the night and move to a motel because they say they've heard such strange things."

The "things" have included mysterious footsteps, banging on doors, and the opening and closing of doors — all at night when no one else was in Glenmore. And although the house was searched thoroughly many times after such occurrences, no rational explanation for the cause was ever forwarded. Said Mrs. Camp: "One guest who hadn't been told about the ghost was taking a nap upstairs and later told us he answered the door four times because he kept hearing knocking. There never was anyone there."

And then there were the inexplicable problems with the swimming pool. "We've had nothing but trouble with that pool since we had it put in," Mrs. Camp declared. "For instance, it is constantly draining. We have had four or five companies come in and try to find out why it drains and where the water goes. Nobody has been able to figure it out."

She thinks, however, she knows why. "'He' probably just got out of his grave one night to take a stroll, walked across where the garden should have been, and fell in the pool." (Psychic experts pretty much agree that ghosts do not like water, and will not even cross a stream or river.) "That probably made 'him' mad enough to make sure we don't get to use it," Mrs. Camp concluded.

A few years ago, the Camps, too, decided to make some changes. The took down the porch that had been added in the late 1800s, and had the entrance stairway moved to the front. "Unknowingly, we were bringing the house back to the way it looked originally," Mrs. Camp said. "I guess the reason 'he' doesn't bother us is because 'he' likes the way we fixed 'his' house up."

Evil in the English Basement

here have been cases, although admittedly rare, in the annals of recorded psychic history where ghosts have literally followed families from house to house, sometimes great distances apart. In terms of spectral phenomena, this is extremely unusual because most spirits are associated with a residence in which they were born and raised, or lived in for a number of years, or suffered some tragic and traumatic experience. In most instances, if the dwelling occupants move, either to get away from the hauntings or for other reasons, they generally leave the ethereal beings behind, some happier at getting rid of the "intruders;" some sadder at losing the company of mortal friends or relatives.

In the few documented occasions where ghosts followed people from one house to another and continued to make their presences known, it usually involved poltergeist-type activity. The spirit had an axe to grind, so to speak, and its "business" was not finished.

Jim and Sue Anne Elmore of Charlottesville must have thought something like this happened to them when they moved from one house to another in the city a few years ago, because extraordinary things happened to them in two separate homes. Yet, as it turned out, this was, in fact, even a rarer event, because there were two *different* sets of ghosts involved, and they were totally unrelated!

It all began in 1978, when the Elmores moved to Albemarle County from Athens, West Virginia, a small town near Bluefield. They bought a house on East Market Street. The original portion of it had been built in the 1820s. "It was one of the largest houses in the neighborhood," says Jim Elmore. "We were about a mile from city hall. It had three floors and an old English basement. There were beautiful flower gardens, and it was in a kind of historic area. Charlottesville's old woolen mills were nearby, as was the river, a graveyard, and railroad tracks. Two major additions had been made to the house; one in the 1880s and one in the 1920s. It was owned for a long time by the Graves family. The elder Mr. Graves had been one of the stockholders in the town's hardware store decades ago.

"We heard stories of Nora Graves, who lived there for a long time. The whole family was sort of eccentric, and one of Nora's brothers went out back one day, laid across the tracks, and was killed by a train," Elmore continues. "In her later years, Nora became sort of reclusive. She spent her last years living in an apartment in the English basement, and she rarely went out. Neighbors told us she was withdrawn and kept mostly to herself. And apparently, she had enough money to live independently. After she died, I think in the early 1970s, the Albemarle Baptist Church bought the house and used it for a while for Sunday School services. We bought it in the spring of 1978 and lived there four years, till the summer of 1982. It was during that time that my wife and I and several of our friends experienced a number of unusual things, and almost all of them happened in the basement."

What were some of the "unusual things?"

"Sue Anne can probably tell you a lot more than I can," Jim says. "She was in the house more. One thing that I will always remember, however, was the cold, icy blast of air you would feel in basement, and it didn't matter what time of year it was, winter or summer. Now, I'm not just talking about a little draft of air coming through a crack in a window or anything like that. These were blasts of air. They would make you stop and take notice. A lot of our friends encountered this as well as us. The other thing I can't forget was the odor. It was indescribable. I don't know how to describe it. It was the foulest, nastiest, most rank smell I ever experienced. It was beyond rotting, organic matter. It would stop you in your tracks, and you would ask yourself, what the hell is that? It was startling. It would only last for a few seconds at a time, but I assure you that was enough."

Jim Elmore also recalls one particular, and frightening manifestation which happened to him one day in the English cellar. "I was walking through the little kitchen down there, on my way outside, when I felt this strong force pushing me. It was like the palm of someone's hand pressed into my back shoving me as hard as it could. I jerked around, but there was no one there. It was very unnerving."

"What I remember specifically about the 'Nora Graves' house, is that we didn't experience any problems until our son, Seth, was born," adds Sue Anne. "That's when I began noticing that awful stench in the basement. It was like rotting, putrid flesh. It was awful, almost like it was a kind of evil spirit oozing up from the center of the earth. I would scrub and scrub and it had no effect. Then it would just disappear. There were a number of times when I had the distinct feeling that I was being ushered out of the basement, and there were a couple of times when I was actually pushed, like Jim. Once, it caused me to trip on my feet. I didn't fall down, but it was definite push. It felt like bony fingers shoving me in the back. Often I had the feeling that there was a presence there. I could feel a current go past me. At first, I was really scared, and then I got indignant."

It was at this point that Sue Anne started reading up on the subject of how to deal with disquieted spirits. "I put lavender, rosemary and distilled extracts around in the basement," she says. "Then we had a conversation with 'Nora.' I told her that we knew she had lived in the house for a long time and that the English basement was her place. But I said that we lived in the house now, and we would have to learn to co-exist. Jim laughed about this. Here we were, grownups, talking to a ghost. But it must have worked, because there was a noticeable quiet after that."

In the summer of 1982, the Elmores moved to a house called Tufton, which was on property that had been part of Thomas Jefferson's Monticello estate. When Jefferson's daughter had to sell off the land to help pay her father's debts, a family named Mason purchased this particular tract and the house is said to have been built in the 1820s or 1830s. The Rivanna River runs through nearby, and Jim calls the area "a lush piece of land." It didn't take long, after moving in, for the Elmores to think that Nora may have moved with them, because spirit-like manifestations began to occur right away. But there seemed to be a difference, and, in time, Jim and Sue Anne realized that there was a whole new set of ghosts at Tufton.

The house is very large, with about 5,000 square feet of living space. The rooms are huge on the first two floors, and there is an attic on the third floor. The "activities" began soon after the Elmores moved in. "It was really curious," says Sue Anne. "I would be in the house and it would be very, very quiet, and I had this sense that I could hear people laboring, like picking up heavy things and moving them. Yet there was no one else in the house. It was not uncommon to hear someone walking in the attic, and then you would hear a door slam. There was a sense of somebody coming through the backside of the house." Jim concurs. "We heard these type noises many times. Doors would open and shut. One night I was upstairs and I thought I heard someone in the kitchen, cooking. I was sure of it, and I assumed it was Sue Anne. I called down from the top of the stairs, and when there was no answer I went down to look. There was no one there."

One of the most unusual occurrences was witnessed by both Jim and Sue Anne. Says Jim: "It was about dusk, and I still can't tell you exactly what it was we saw. It was standing in the main hall when we first saw it. It was an amber colored figure moving in the back of the house. It literally shimmered. I had the strangest feeling. And as it moved, there were intense, laboring footsteps, like it was carrying something very heavy. It appeared to be human-like, and yet it wasn't human. I don't quite know how to describe it. It walked through the hallway and did not seem to be in any hurry or anything, It was just like a friend of yours would walk by you. At first, I didn't believe that I saw it, then I realized that I did see it."

"I believe it was a male," says Sue Anne. "It apparently had come up from the basement. It was in full color. It was amber and it was in a shape that was not well defined, but it seemed to be the shape of a person. It was awesome, but for some reason I was not at all frightened by it. We were mind blown. Neither Jim or I said a word. We were speechless. It took your breath away. We just stared. It moved by us and appeared to be going outside, paying no attention to us. The hair raised on my arms and I had goosebumps all over."

Sue Anne also had another extraordinary experience at Tufton. She had done some research on the house and believed that it had been occupied at one time, perhaps while Thomas Jefferson was still alive, by indentured servants. Sue Anne thinks they were white servants, and possible house servants at Monticello. She isn't sure. "A lot of people lived in that place and they left a lot of spiritual activity behind," she says.

"I was alone in the house one day. I remember it was very hot, and I was carrying a load of clothes up the stairs. There was no air conditioning. About half way up the stairs I stopped, leaned against the wall, and shut my eyes for a moment. I felt a very strong presence. I mean *very* strong! I don't know how to put it in words. This may sound crazy, but it was as if I had slipped into a time warp, and I became that presence; I became another person. It was the presence of a young girl, a servant or a slave. I think she was either white or mulatto. She, or I, was wearing an old muslin type dress. It was gray and had no buttons. It wasn't fancy at all, maybe like a uniform, with a fitted bodice and long sleeves.

"It was like a feeling of regression, like I had gone back in time and assumed this person's body. Although she was young, I felt that she was worn out. She had had too many children, and she had been worked too hard. There was an overwhelming sense of weariness of her body. I felt the total sadness and tiredness of that young woman. I felt her smallness and her utter fatigue, so much so, in fact, that I didn't have the strength to carry the clothes upstairs. I don't know how long I stood there on the stairs. It might have been four or five minutes. And then the feeling lifted, and I was back in present time again. I had a feeling of astonishment. It was so real."

CHAPTER 10

A Sampling of Spectral Vignettes

* * * * *

THE HAUNTING HESSIAN

ometimes it doesn't pay to taunt a ghost! A dinner guest once laughed at Dot Boulware, owner of Edgewood, a quaint Victorian manor home on Route 5 between Richmond and Williamsburg, when told of the resident spirit there, a lovelorn Miss Lizzie. "You don't believe all that nonsense," the guest said. Perhaps by coincidence, but at that precise instant a copper plate hanging on the wall fell off and banged the skeptical woman on the top of her head. She abruptly left the house.

A somewhat similar incident was reported in an 18th century home in the Charlottesville area in the 1970s, although the name of the house and its location were never revealed because the owners didn't want it known. The story here was that a Hessian mercenary soldier during the Revolutionary War time tried to force entry into the house and the owner shot him in the face. In 1976, the owner of the house was showing a guest the Hessian soldier's grave, and he told him how the man had been killed, and how he periodically came back apparently still seeking entry.

The guest, admitting he didn't believe a word of the story, started dancing on the grave, and taunted, "come out, Hessian, come out!" When nothing happened immediately, he laughed. However, half an hour later, when he was walking alone across a broad lawn near the house, he said, "I felt a strange presence hovering over my shoulder and heard very heavy breathing. I was afraid to turn around. The breathing got heavier and heavier until it was almost screaming in my ear. Terrified, I turned abruptly, saw that God-awful inflamed face, and ran into the house." He said he had been so scared, it took him a long while before he could tell his hosts what had happened.

It is a shame that this property remains anonymous, because it seemed to be rife with ghostly phenomena. One owner reported that just after moving in, "while we were lying in bed, we heard a loud stamping of footsteps on the porch leading to the back door. The door opened, the steps proceeded inside the house, and the next thing we knew our bedroom door opened with a whoosh. A strong warm breeze poured in the room and rippled the bed sheets. Four or five seconds later, our door closed, then the back door closed, and we heard the loud steps trudge back down the porch. It was," he under-stated, "a somewhat unnerving experience."

Yet a third haunting occurred in a tenant house on the grounds, built about 1820. It was the alleged scene of a grisly murder some-time after the Civil War. A man had killed his wife there. A young couple rented the house in the 1970s and every two or three months they heard "nightmare screams" of a woman rip through the house. The wife related the experience: "The previous tenants had told us about the murder story and the screaming. . . the first time I person-ally heard the scream was one afternoon when I was cooking in the kitchen. It was extremely loud. My husband was reading in the next room, but, strangely, he didn't hear a thing. We learned since then that the murdered woman can only be heard in the kitchen."

Later, when the house was sold, the new owner decided not to take any chances. She had the entire estate exorcised, and the spec-tral happenings ceased.

* * * * *

STRANGE SOUNDS AT HAWKWOOD

Right from the first after Susan Jofko and her roommate moved into the two-century-old tenant house on the Green Springs estate of Hawkwood in Louisa County in the mid 1970s, strange things began to happen. On her first evening in the place, for example, she was awakened in the mid-dle of the night by footsteps going up and down the steps and walk-ing around the hall. "I knew they were footsteps because of their regularity and the person sounded like he was wearing shoes." She rushed out to see who it was. "I saw nothing."

This happened night after night. Then she told of doors opening when no one else was home. Next came the soft music. "It would come from the kitchen," Susan said, "but when I would get there it would stop. It sounded like a flute. It wasn't very loud but very distinct. In time, Susan began to wonder if was just her. But then one night a friend was over, and after dinner they started a fire and closed the door of the living room to keep the heat from escaping.

"We started talking about the 'ghost'," Susan remembers, "and he laughed and said, rather loudly, that there was no such thing as a ghost." At that moment, the latched door to the living room swung partly open and then closed and latched itself! "My friend's mouth dropped and his eyes bugged out," Susan says. "I've never seen anyone so scared. I was nervous, but by then I was more used to it all. I just tried to comfort him by saying it was the wind. But we both knew it couldn't have been the wind."

The manifestations continued. Often, Susan's dog, a Rhodesian Ridgeback, seemed to sense a presence in the house. Susan said he would growl and act as if he could see or hear something. She couldn't. Once when she was alone in the kitchen, the back porch door opened and swung back "like someone was walking across the porch." The door to the house opened several seconds later and closed shut. One night a young landscape architect came over to show a stained glass window. He placed it in a bathroom window and all the lights in the house, except for that bathroom, were turned off. They then stepped out on the front lawn to see the stained glass. "As we looked at it," Susan says, we saw a shadow of a man pass in front of the light. I ran into the house to see if I could catch whoever or whatever it was. Nothing."

Susan says she did not find any comfort in concluding that she shared the old tenant house with a spirit. "If someone were to give me some explanations to the things that have been going on out here, I would not be at all upset to find out that I don't have a ghost. But right now I have no other answers."

* * * * *

PLEASE DON'T DIG UP MY GRAVE

here is at least one recorded incident, as reported by "Virginia Ghosts" author Margaret DuPont Lee and others, of a woman ghost returning from her final resting place to ask that those still living in the area not disturb her grave site. Sounds like a reasonable request.

This particular phenomena appeared before Mrs. J. P. Walters, who lived at a house called Newington, at Mountain Run, Orange County. It may have been built as early as 1758, or even before. Mrs. Walters had not been in the house long when she asked an old man who had worked there for 15 years if he would clear a patch of unsightly land, "overgrown by bushes in the garden back of the graveyard." He told her it couldn't be done, because he had tried to plow that land a number of times, and every time he did, strange things happened, and the mules would sink down in old grave sites every few steps.

Nevertheless, some time later, Mrs. Walters ordered some plowing done in the garden itself, and as this was being done, the horse sank into a deep cavity. A little digging led to a grave containing a skeleton.

That night, Mrs. Walters was awakened in bed at about 11 p.m., first by an inexplicable noise, and then by the visionary figure of a tall, gaunt woman standing at the foot of her bed. She had a high forehead, thin lips and large, deep blue eyes. She looked like a living mortal, other than for the sickening pallor of her chalky skin. Before she could scream, the apparition told her not to be afraid. She said her name was Ethel Cavanaugh and that she had lived at Newington long before the Sanford family had been there, and they had moved in about 1840.

Managing to recover her nerve, Mrs. Walters told the figure she had never seen her grave in the enclosed lot, and the woman said that she had died in the room above the spiral stairway and the had been buried in the garden, years before the current cemetery had been set aside. She then asked if she could be laid back to rest in her grave and left alone in peace. It was a request Mrs. Walters was only too pleased to grant.

* * * * *

THE GHOSTLY NUT CRACKER

t is said that Miss Betsy Maury had a great predilection for black walnuts. It is said that she could sit by the fireplace at night and crack and eat walnuts for hours at a time. It is said by some that Betsy still cracks the walnuts at a house called Midmont, near the University of Virginia campus. If she indeed does, a lot of people would find this rather peculiar and difficult to explain in that she died well over a century ago!

Betsy was the sister of Thomas Walker Maury, a member of the Virginia Legislature and a friend of Thomas Jefferson. She moved into Midmont with her brother about 1830, and both of them were considered just a little bit eccentric. In time, Betsy became engaged and she sailed to Paris, France, to buy her trousseau, but something unknown happened and the marriage never took place. She wore the clothes she bought overseas for the rest of her life.

When her brother married a local widow and moved out, Betsy bought Midmont from him and lived there alone for the rest of her life. It is reported that when she went out, she wore a sunbonnet to avoid students who teased her. She died in the house, and ever since, the sounds of cracking walnuts can sometimes be heard in a downstairs room. "I've heard the cracking noises many times," said Charlottesville attorney and Midmont owner Bernard Chamberlain in a newspaper interview in 1976. No shells are ever found, however. Ghosts are the neatest people!

* * * * *

EERIE EVENTS AT ELKTON

And things that go bump in the night! You would think that a police department would be a nice, safe and cozy place to work, right? Not according to Hilda Meadows, a night dispatcher for the Elkton Police Department in Rockingham County, northwest of Charlottesville. She was working the four to midnight shift one evening in 1981 when things got quiet so she decided to take advantage of the break and go to the bathroom down the hall.

She describes what happened next: "It was when I opened the door to come out that I first heard it. It was a terrible moaning. I mean there was something in that building somewhere. I don't know how to describe what I heard, but I don't ever want to hear anything like it again. I started running back down the hall toward the dispatcher's office, and I could hear the moaning overtop my head like it was following me. But as soon as I opened the door to the office, it quit all of a sudden. That's when I saw the calendar in the office moving. It was swinging back and forth like the wind had a hold of it. But there wasn't any wind in here. Then it stopped, and nobody touched it."

On subsequent nights both she and fellow dispatcher Margie Green heard footsteps directly above their office when no one else was in the building. Some of the police officers suggested it might be the pipes in the old antebellum building, but Hilda doesn't buy it. "I'd like them to have heard what I've heard and say it's the pipes!" Margie Green agrees. She heard the footsteps at least half a dozen times and once she and a police officer rushed upstairs to see if it was a prankster. They found no one in the building and the doors and windows were bolted. Yet as soon as Margie returned to the dispatcher's office in the basement of the building, the footsteps began again. They came from the room she and the officer had just searched. "You tell me what I heard," Margie said. "I wish someone would."

It should be added that the old two story brick house, which was renovated to accommodate Elkton's municipal offices, once served as a hospital during the Civil War. The basement, where the police department is, was the morgue.

* * * * *

A SPIRIT NAMED MAX

For years, residents at the unassuming, box-like house at 537 Layman Avenue in Harrisonburg — many of them students at James Madison University — reported hearing a wide assortment of strange noises at all hours of the night. There were the all-too-familiar footsteps up and down the stairs; "shuffling" sounds outside bedroom doors; and moans and groans from no apparent human source.

In an effort to tap the root cause of such incidents, the home owners called in a medium and a "spiritual encounter" was held. According to witnesses, in the midst of the seance, a male voice with a thick German accent was heard. He introduced himself as Max, and he told those present that he "remained" in the house to protect it from the "greedy clutches of his sister's ghost."

Max, through the medium, was said to have said that as he lay dying, his sister tried to "doctor" his last will and testament so that the house would be left to her. Max knew she was doing this but was too weak to stop her. That is why, he added, that after his death he has stayed on, and why real-life occupants often hear noises they cannot account for. He could not stop his sister from fulfilling her evil intentions in life, so he tarried after death to set things right.

The Spiritual Vision
of Swannanoa

I f ever there were a place that one might suspect to be haunted, it likely would be the colossal, 52-room Italian Renaissance marble mansion, Swannanoa, which sits majestically atop Afton Mountain near Rockfish Gap, near the city of Waynesboro, west of Charlottesville. And, indeed, one could find ample cause for spiritual intervention there, even if hard evidence of psychic manifestations are difficult to come by. There are strong indications of the powers of premonition at work here, rumors of clandestine visits by international celebrities, a hint at supernatural happenings, and also the report of a ghostly photograph.

The huge palace-like structure itself is demanding of attention in its own right. Around 1911, Major James Dooley, a millionaire lawyer and financial wizard from Richmond, bought a large tract of land atop Afton Mountain, and shortly thereafter began construction of Swannanoa, supposedly named by his wife for a native tribe of Indians. (In Indian, Swannanoa means "Land of Beauty," and by its East Indian name — in Sanskrit — "The Absolute," or "The Mother of Heaven.") It should be noted here that Major Dooley is the same gentleman who built the Maymont estate, now a popular park in Richmond. The mansion there is said to be haunted by the ghost of a young woman, as was detailed in the author's book, "The Ghosts of Richmond."

Just carrying the materials for the palatial giant Swannanoa up the mountain 80-odd years ago, must have been a monumental task. The building is constructed of Georgia marble outside, and Italian Carrara and Sienna marble inside, and is complete with rare wood carvings, mural paintings, a $100,000 Tiffany stained glass window, a beautiful marble double staircase, and a domed ceiling. There is, too, a vast baronial hall — "fit for the entertainment of kings" — surrounded by a gold tapestried ballroom, a library and an oak paneled dining room. Not surprisingly, it took an army of 300 master artisans eight years to build the mansion — for a cost of $1 million. Today, it would cost 20 to 50 times that amount. The adjacent garden is terraced three tiers high with marble steps and terrace walls, and a marvelous marble columned, rose covered pergola, which "is a joy and marvel to all who meditate in its poetic shades. Swannanoa, which is open to the public, has been called a "shrine of beauty."

Major and Mrs. Dooley both died in the 1920s, and the estate was sold and resold several times in the years prior to World War II. President and Mrs. Calvin Coolidge, the first of many world famous visitors, spent a Thanksgiving holiday there during his administration. Several attempts were made to convert the house and grounds into a lavish country club, but the costs of maintenance and operation were so great these proved unsuccessful although there is a golf course there today.

It was during these years that Dooley's mountain paradise deteriorated into "jungle ruin . . . for 20 years the prey of the weather and vandals." It was at this point, in the early 1940s, that incidents of premonitionary vision came into being. Enter Dr. Walter Russell and his extraordinary wife, Lao. Dr. Russell has been described as a "sculptor, painter, architect, composer, author, philosopher and doctor of science. . . . internationally known as the American Leonardo (da Vinci) and the most versatile man in America." Lao was an author, philosopher, sculptor and scientist. She also, apparently, was a visionary. A brochure on Swannanoa says that "in her spiritual consciousness she saw the illumined Jesus looking ecstatically upward into the night from a high pinnacle on God's *Sacred Mountain*."

The brochure also says Lao Russell was "an illumined messenger of the Light (Jesus had said 'God is Light')" and that she was "destined from birth to interpret the Light for other men. For many days the inspiration of this ecstatic vision illumined her very soul." She then told her husband, "Come, we must leave this city forever and find God's Sacred Mountain. God will lead us to it."

There upon the couple set out on a long, arduous search for the site she had seen in her vision. They travelled across the country, looking high into the Rocky Mountains, the Sierras and other great ranges of the West. They looked at Mt. Rainier, Mt. Hood, Mt. Shasta and Pike's Peak "questioningly, as though awaiting the fulfillment of a greater destiny than to be just some majestic pile of grandeur for

tourists to see." Walter Russell noted later, "We meditated long in the Garden of the Gods but from none of these many mountains of the West did Lao hear God's Voice say, 'This is The Sacred Mountain,' nor did she recognize in any of them the mountain of her vision."

Then as summer was ending, Lao suddenly said, "Come, we shall go to the Blue Ridge Mountains of the South where I first so strongly felt the urge to go." Walter Russell then told what happened; "Forthwith, we obeyed the ever loudening Inner Voice, and in due time found ourselves on the ridge of Swannanoa's mountain. And as we looked out over the two great North-South valleys toward range after range of blue mountains, then upward toward the highest point of the mountain above them, Lao reverently said, 'This is the place God brought me to — *this* is the Sacred Mountain of my vision'." The year was 1948.

Lao Russell has written that strange things have happened at Swannanoa. "I have heard from one woman in the valley below our mountain that on a certain night when she was a child, the mountain was covered with light. It turned out that this was the same night that I was born in England, thousands of miles away," she has said.

"On three different occasions, a rainbow has descended out of the heavens straight down to the top of the palace. On one of these occasions, I had been ill for weeks from a smallpox vaccination, and had been experiencing terrible fevers. On the night the rainbow appeared, I received an immediate healing."

Lao also wrote about a "Godly vision" she had shortly after taking up residence at Swannanoa. "Three weeks after we came, one of the pipes underneath the basement rotted out and we were completely without water. The plumbers gave us an estimate of $50,000 to dig up the basement and find the pipe. It was money we did not have. I said to Dr. Russell, 'God brought us to the mountain and I asked Him to show us where the leak was.' At 3:30 or 4:00 in the morning, God gave me a vision of where the broken pipe was. The workmen thought I was crazy, but they gave me a quote of $84.50 to dig up the one spot I showed them. I had them dig it up. They couldn't believe it, but the broken pipe was right where I had told them."

It was thus here, over the next few years, that the talented couple merged their creative geniuses to develop the "University of Science and Philosophy." In a bulletin-announcement of the purpose and objective of this unusual, perhaps unique institution, it says, "The outstanding value of the University . . . can better be understood by asking yourself how many thousands of average humans it would take to balance the value of one Rachmaninoff, or one Beethoven, Leonardo or Laotzu. Or whether all of the automobiles ever manufactured could equal in value one Michaelangelo, Lizst or Phideas.

"One can better comprehend the power of one who is cosmic minded over one who is not, by realizing that during all time there have been comparatively few great Illuminates and geniuses, while, during the same period, there have been more than 100 billion other humans. When you consider that there were but a few each century, and that all the great and enduring beauty of the ages came from those few, it is not difficult to realize that one genius is worth more to the world than 100,000 average men, and one Illuminate is worth many millions of men. The tragedy is that we have not learned the value of such supermen, and that our habit is to suppress and crucify them, instead of glorify them. If you think of human values in this light you will realize the great need of a university for aiding man to become aware of his inner powers."

The university has no formal student body, per se. Rather, it is a center for meditation and inspiration. States the bulletin: "Reading, writing and arithmetic can be taught to groups, but the inner Light of man cannot be awakened that way. Mass teachings reach the brain

Statue of Christ of the Blue Ridge at Swannanoa

of man through his senses but cosmic inspiration comes to man only when he has become enabled to sever the seat of sensation in his brain from the seat of Consciousness in his pineal gland, that minute portion of the body which has mystified the medical profession for centuries. Such a severance is possible at any time, anywhere, but rarely comes to any man or woman except in seclusion and in deep meditation.

"Just as it is necessary for a Beethoven to seek seclusion, in order to write a Moonlight Sonata, so is it equally necessary for a searcher of the Source of inspiration to seek solitude to study our teachings, which lead to cosmic power."

"And thus," says the brochure, "was Lao's vision fulfilled. . . The many who journey there daily tell of the wonders they beheld and how they carried away with them something deep and wondrous beyond words or sight — a new power — perhaps they, too, glimpsed Lao's vision and knew that Love's symbol had again come to spread the Light of God's Word to all mankind."

According to at least two of Afton Mountain's long-time residents — neighbors of the palace and university at Swannanoa — there have been many other curious visits to the Shrine of Beauty over the years. According to an article in the Washington Post in early 1992, William Bennett Edwards, owner of the Gold Rush Gun Shop on Skyline Drive, and his wife, Virginia Davis Edwards, many of the world's leading luminaries have come here. They say they have seen Ted Kennedy, Jackie Kennedy Onassis, the Queen of England, Pope John Paul II, Spiro Agnew, Gerald Ford, Margaret Thatcher, Elizabeth Taylor, Lady Bird Johnson, H. R. Haldeman, Idi Amin, and "CIA and corporate big shots" drive by their place and enter the grounds of Swannanoa. They say that Henry Kissinger is a regular visitor.

Edwards told the Washington Post reporter that he was convinced Swannanoa is owned by the royal family of England and "serves as the secret meeting place of the agents of the Council of 30 — supposedly an all-powerful cadre that has manipulated world economies, incited wars and ordered assassinations for its own financial advantage throughout recorded history." Adds Mrs. Edwards: "Little by little we put it together. We finally figured something really big was going on."

Edwards, described by the reporter as "an intelligent and seemingly reasonable man," noted, "I can't say there's evidence," but he remains steadfastly convinced that he has "uncovered a conspiracy of international and millennial dimensions that is unfolding right outside his door."

And, finally, there are the two possible incidents of actual psychic phenomena that are said to have happened on the mountain top. One involves the Russell's masterpiece, a 30-foot high model of The Christ of the Blue Ridge. Lao Russell once said that "we must fulfill my vision by creating . . . a glorious figure of Jesus. This . . . must depict a man of great physical strength — for the glorious figure of my vision was twice my size and His head was uplifted with the power of God's ecstasy and somehow one could *feel* His great strength. I remember His hands on my shoulders felt like the boughs of a tree — so strong and big were they. And His brow was broad and high and the jaw strong and determined. His eyes, although tender and full of great love, were also filled with the fire of great purpose. Oh, but the sculptural figure we must do of Jesus must be a magnificent one rising high into the heavens above the highest point of the mountain." There is an unsubstantiated yet recurring story that a large bird flew into this very statue once during a furious storm, and the figure was seen bleeding from the heart!

And, lastly, there are the inexplicable photographs! Sometime late in the 1970s three Polaroid pictures were taken of Lao Russell on the double marble staircase, producing a mystical manifestation. In her words: "The three pictures are difficult to describe for I have never seen anything like them before or since. A man was taking a picture of his wife standing beside me on the double marble staircase. She had a white dress on and is prematurely whiteheaded. The gentleman had taken two or three pictures, which he informed us were not coming out, and was crushing them and putting them into his pocket.

"I said, 'Do let me see the one you have just taken!' When I looked at it, my heart jumped for joy, for there superimposed on his wife's body and head was my Beloved's body! In place of her white hair was a dark beret and covering her white dress was a brightly colored coat such as Dr. Russell liked to wear. The two previous pictures he had crushed showed light rays — one stronger than the other — coming into focus on the woman's body. I have known my Oneness with my Beloved from the time of his refolding, but this was the only time that I have ever had a picture or seen a presence. One needs only one such experience to know the everlasting comfort of our eternal Oneness with those we love."

There is one other brief footnote. William Edwards says the Swannanoa mansion was built on the precise site where eight Jesuit missionaries were killed by Indians more than 300 years ago!

CHAPTER 12

The Legendary Moon Ghost of Scottsville

or 74 years, 'Echoes of the Moon Ghost' have resounded from our low-lying hills to the beautiful Blue Ridge Mountains of Virginia, and on to places far beyond. These echoes have persisted, not alone because interest attaches to an unsolved mystery, but mostly because, as a manifestation of the social unrest and insecurity of a crucial period, the story of the so-called 'Moon Ghost' belongs to the history and folklore of Albemarle County, and therefore to the ages and to all of the people."

This is how Frances Moon Butts began her reading of a paper before the Albemarle County Historical Society on July 24, 1940. The paper covered her recollections — as recounted to her by her father, by other members of the Moon family, and by servants and other "live" witnesses — of one of the most extraordinary, and most widely publicized ghost stories in the annals of Virginia.

Surprisingly, very little is known about the legendary "Moon Ghost" of Scottsville today. In fact, in 1930, when Margaret DuPont Lee published her classic book, "Virginia Ghosts," no mention was made of this bizarre episode. Yet, 125 years ago when the Scottsville Register ran a detailed account of the strange happenings which occurred at John Schuyler Moon's house over a sustained two year period, the news caused a sensation. The newspaper, said Frances Moon Butts, Moon's niece, "sold like 'War Specials' in Richmond, and the Packet Boat came for more! Reprints were made and still Lynchburg and other places clamored for papers." One writer, in summing up the sequence of events noted that "Scottsville's peaceful image was badly blemished . . . bringing national fame to that once sleepy town."

Not only were people all over the Commonwealth clamoring for more information about the on-going escapades of the alleged spirit, but thousands of them streamed into the small town from all directions in hopes of personally witnessing a slice of psychic phenomena. At one point, for example, about 25 University of Virginia students decided to venture over to Scottsville and keep a midnight vigil at the Moon residence. During the night they were not disappointed. It is said that when they saw, or thought they saw, a "mysterious shape" on the roof of the house, "15 guns fired in vain." Detectives and psychic experts from as far away as Washington, D.C. came to the area and literally camped out "many long nights" waiting to observe the specter.

It got so out of hand, wrote Frances Butts, that "my uncle, a man of dignity and reserve, seems to have been more resentful of the exaggerated publicity the ghost brought than of its almost nightly depredations. He finally refused to let anything be published that he did not write."

Though the incredible running series of manifestations occurred from August 1866 to 1868, the mystery of the Moon Ghost has never been satisfactorily solved. In fact, even today, there remains a larger, overriding question: was it a ghost at all? Or was it a vengeful human being, or more than one person? As Moon's niece put it in her talk in 1940, "The details of nearly everything the ghost is said to have done are equally controversial, and contradictory."

There is no question that the events happened. They were described and documented in detail, and in most instances, they were witnessed by more than one member of the family, and in many instances they were witnessed by large numbers of people. The question is were these events staged by an ethereal presence or by a living man or men.

A reasonable argument can be made for the latter possibility. It was during the reconstruction period when the nation was still recovering from the great wounds of the Civil War. Conditions were unsettled. One President of the United States had been assassinated and another one nearly impeached. Frances Butts said "the newly-freed slaves, untrained to habits of self-support, were mostly unemployed, often unrestrained. . . . Even justice was irrational and often severe."

She adds that her uncle was a lawyer and that he once defended a neighbor who had been attacked by an armed intruder. Apparently, he was successful, because Mrs. Butts said, "when driven away, this negro left vowing vengeance on my uncle." John

Moon also was successful in the conviction of Lucian Beard, a notorious leader of a horse-thief gang. After the ghostly episodes finally ended, Beard wrote Moon from the penitentiary in Richmond and offered to explain the ghost if Moon would secure his pardon. Moon never answered him.

Could the ghost, in reality, have been either the vengeful intruder or perhaps one of Beard's gang of rowdies. That would make sense. But then again, could that person, or persons, have sustained a series of events over a two year period, which included penetration of the Moon house on a continuous basis, sometimes every night for weeks at a time? Could such a person have eluded scores of gunmen who kept watch at night during this period? Many times the house and grounds were ringed solid with family members, neighbors, law officers and the just plain curious. Could such a person have escaped the gunfire aimed at them on numerous occasions? It is reported that more than once bullets found their marks on the mystery trespasser, but each time he bounded up immediately and eluded posses of men chasing him. How would one explain this?

Perhaps it is best, at this point, to examine some of the specific occurrences, so readers may judge for themselves. Preceding the beginning of the ghostly manifestations, one Sunday morning in the summer of 1866, someone banged on the front door of John Moon's estate, known as Church Hill, five miles north of Scottsville. Two "rough men" demanded to see the head of the house. A grandson explained that Moon had gone to church. The strangers then "whirled away on their mounts." Some neighbors saw them ride in the direction of a nearby graveyard. When Moon returned, he and some friends rode off around the neighborhood in search of the two men, but never found them. Shortly after that, the Moon Ghost began appearing.

The specifics of the intrusions were covered in graphic detail in a long article in the Scottsville Register issue of November 11, 1867, more than a year after the phenomena started. The article was written by J. L. Brandy, editor of the Register, and it was headlined, "The Mysterious Affair at the Residence of Mr. J. S. Moon." The article was reprinted five days later in the Charlottesville Chronicle, and a copy of this is on file at the Alderman Library of the University of Virginia.

The following excerpts were taken from this edition. The article began with a preamble:

"Our readers are aware that we have heretofore studiously avoided publishing anything in connection with what has occurred at the residence of Mr. John S. Moon, (five miles from our town,) during the past few months. Mr. Moon is a lawyer by profession, and has quite an extensive practice; but while he is well known to the public in this respect, it is exceedingly unpleasant to him to have a notoriety forced upon him by the remarkable circumstances related below.

"If the mysteries are kept up, we will make a weekly report; and the reader may rest assured that we will state nothing but what is strictly true. A matter so serious should, and shall be, by us, handled seriously and truthfully."

And then editor Brady began his article under a Scottsville dateline: "About ten months ago, a candle box, filled with rags saturated with whiskey was placed against a side of Mr. J. S. Moon's house, five miles from this place, and ignited. About 1 o'clock at night the fire was discovered and extinguished; and the unburnt rags discovered to be fragments of garments missing from Mr. Moon's house, in the then past several months. Whether this effort to burn the house had any connection with what has followed, is not known.

"Mr. Moon was not again molested that he is aware of, until Spring opened, when a member of his family saw a man standing motionless a few feet in front of his house at night. On another occasion two men were seen to walk back and forth across the yard.

"On another occasion a Negro woman reported she saw a black looking man crouched at Mr. Moon's front gate, late at night; and on another occasion, also late at night, a similar looking man was seen crouched near the gate, who afterwards got up and went towards the house.

"During Mr. Moon's absence, attending court, about that time, his parlor door which had been carefully shut and locked (the key being left in the lock at night) was found open in the morning.

"In a night or so afterwards, a parlor window which had been fixed with a straw stuck in a crack of it, was found to have been heisted; the store room door was found open, (unaccountably), several mornings about that time.

"After this, Mr. M. fixed his inside and outside doors and windows in such a way as to know if they were disturbed, and found they were repeatedly opened. He watched on the inside of his house for a good many nights nearly all night, but failed to detect any one attempting to enter. No one disturbed the house the nights he watched.

"One night, about six weeks ago, Mr. M. fastened all doors and windows carefully. He was the first one to get up the next morning, and found his inside dining room door had been opened — a store room door opening into the dining room had been unlocked and opened — a door opening into the kitchen from the dining room had also been unlocked and opened, and the sliding kitchen door had been moved back. A light had been seen to flash about the house that night after the family had all retired. From the store room about four or five pounds of sugar, gotten and weighed that evening, had been taken, and the whiskey out of a demijohn known to have been full the night before, was missing. By the sugar was a basket of silverware which was not disturbed.

"The next night Mr. Moon's son, about 14 years old, was sleeping in his father's office, which is about 100 yards from the house. On this night an effort was made to hoist the window, which awakened his son. He jumped up, saw a man run off, got his gun and made ineffectual pursuit.

"The next night some one was heard to stumble on an open shed over the back passage door — a loud crash immediately followed. Upon going out, Mr. Moon found on the ground, not far from the shed several ladies and children's garments, taken from the upper part of the house and the remains of two plates taken from the dining room, wrapped up in them — also a Bible taken from the dining room mantle piece a few feet off. A child's bonnet wrapped up in a roll of children's clothes was found on top of the shed.

"The next night was dark, windy and rainy. About midnight a pane of glass in one of the dining room windows was smashed in, and the sash raised. Some one was heard to jump in, and when the alarm was given, to jump out again — no one was seen.

"The next night was windy and dark, and the rain fell in torrents. Every door and window was carefully closed by Mr. Moon except the back passage door, and he placed all of his family in his chamber — in a room opening next to him. He sat in this open door with his gun in his hand about two hours, when suddenly the window around the corner from his was busted in with a loud crash. He rushed to the spot, but could not have seen or heard a man moving in three feet of him on account of the darkness, wind and rain, and the outcry of his family. He then closed, and locked the door in the room in which he sat, and in order to keep from being seen against the sky, crawled around to the front of the house, and placed himself 20 yards in front of his front door, where he remained until about day. While there he heard the rattle of a sash of glass, but could see nothing for the darkness. In the morning, he found that the putty around a side light to this front door next to the lock, had been cut out, evidently with the intention of unlocking the door. An effort, which was nearly successful, had also been made to force in the side light sashes and the panels below them.

"The next day was clear, and Mr. Moon made arrangements for eight of his neighbors to surround the house about half an hour after the moon went down, which it did that night about 11 o'clock. If anyone entered the house, it was understood that Mrs. Moon, at one of the windows upstairs, and one of sisters at the other, were to raise signal lights. Mr. Moon retired to his chamber in his usual way, so as to deceive the burglar, and locking the door, extinguishing the light, and rustling the bed clothes, sat with his gun in his hand. A short time after the moon went down, soft footsteps were heard in his parlor, but the wind was blowing, and the sound might have been deceptive. His son crept down, and peeping into the dining room, saw that a window had been hoisted. Upon going back and reporting, the ladies doubted the report. He went down a second time, satisfied himself fully, and coming back, it was determined he should shoot the rogue as he went out of the open window.

"In a few minutes he saw a man about 20 steps from the house and fired on him. The signal lights went up — the man fell flat and crept off. At the same instant that young Moon fired, a man ran between two of the guards, about 200 yards off, on the other side of the yard, and was fired at by one of them with a pistol. The other guard could not fire for fear of shooting one of his companions. The next morning tracks made by a coarse boot, or shoe, were found coursing down the hill from that point. That night the store room door was found locked, but upon going in they found a bag, with two apartments to it, left on the flour barrel, and about a double handful of coffee spilt in with the flour. A shawl, missing from the dining room, was dropped at the spot Mr. Moon's son shot at the man. It seemed to have been perforated with three shots. The entrance and exit of the thief had evidently been made through the back passage door by means of a false key, although the door was found locked. The window had been hoisted to escape through in case Mr. Moon came out of his chamber. The thief was disturbed by the whispering upstairs.

"The next night it was determined to let the rogue come in, if he would, and try to shoot him in the house. Mr. Moon's brother stood gun in hand in the back part of the passage — two other gentlemen were in the house to relieve or assist him, if necessary. Late at night, by moonlight, a man was observed from an upstairs window, crawling cautiously by a flower border from the front gate. It seemed to take him nearly half an hour to reach the house. He had in his hand a long rod, which was supposed to be a ram rod. Approaching near to the house he seemed to prefer exposing the front part of his person and crawled with his back to the ground. Upon reaching the foundation of the house, he reached around with his rod and smashed a side light in the face of Mr. Moon's brother who immediately fired through the door, under the mistaken impression that he was about to enter the house. He was observed to move off rapidly, but with his body kept very near to the ground. The side light selected to break was one through which the door could be unlocked, with the key left in the lock every night. The same night he was seen on the outskirts of the yard again.

"The next night there were 14 men around the house — two of them, however, made a gap by leaving their posts early in the night. Mr. Moon's brother was on duty about 60 yards directly in front. At a late hour he heard someone step boldly on the platform before the front door and unlock the door and go in. He supposed it was some member of the family. One of the ladies upstairs heard a noise below and awoke Mr. Moon's son. She afterwards saw a man go out of the front door and crouch by the side of the platform. Mr. Moon's son went to the window and fired down at the spot she indicated. The guards rushed to the house and found as they supposed that night, a large blood stain on the steps, over which they exulted very much. Fruitless pursuit was made. The men came in and had hardly gotten quiet, when signal whistles, frequently repeated, were heard in various directions from the house. In the morning, Mr. Moon had reason to question whether the stain on the step was blood or not; but had no means of determining its character.

"The next night there were three men on guard about the house. One of them stationed at the yard fence, reports that he saw a man rise up from among a clump of bushes and walk off a short distance and take a position as if to watch the house. He fired at him with a shotgun. The man, he says, fell immediately. He fired again at the spot where he fell. There was no result from this shooting. Mr. Moon's impression is that the object shot at, fell just before the first shot, or it may have been a man with defensive armor on.

"The next night there were 10 or 12 men around the house. Two of them reported that they saw a man creeping on all fours along the garden fence — one of them shot at him with a pistol without result. At a later hour they saw the same object, and made chase, but he escaped among the grape vines and high weeds nearby.

"For some few nights the moon shone nearly all night and the family were not disturbed. Mr. Moon ventured to leave home to attend the Albemarle Circuit Court, his neighbors volunteered to protect his family.

"Upon returning from Albemarle Court on the next Saturday night, a neighbor came in to spend the night. Before retiring Mr. Moon put him in charge of the main body of the house. He fastened every door and window carefully. Mr. Moon in going out of the back passage door to his chamber, locked the door on the inside and left the key in the door to prevent a false key from being put in the lock. This night young Moon slept at the office, the first time for eight or ten nights. He says he had not time to go to sleep before the dog began to bark on the other side of the yard, and he heard someone walking around. He heard also the clank of metal which he described to be such as soldiers make when having sabres attached to them. The man kept close to the foundation of the house, but made a good deal of noise, as if he wished to attract the attention of the dog. About an hour before day, young Moon succeeded to catch a glimpse of him through the window, and fired at him, but lodged nearly his whole load in a chair which had been fixed against the window . . . . The report of young Moon's gun frightened whoever it was, and he ran out at the back door, leaving it open.

"The next week Mr. Moon was compelled to attend court again. After an interval of several nights, which two of Mr. Moon's neighbors were inside watching the front door, someone came to it and struck forcibly on the door or sill, from appearances, seen through the side and top lights, most probably with the butt end of a musket. The first strike aroused the whole family. One of the men fired through he door at him. Mr. Moon's sister-in-law saw him from an upper window, run around the corner of the house and pause to peep back to see if he was pursued. She fired at him twice from the window, which was open, with a little pocket pistol. He fell to the ground (at) the first fire, and moved off after some hesitation. The men rushed out in wrong directions to hunt for him. He was seen in the yard again that night.

"The next night Mr. Moon's sister-in-law saw from the closet window a tall man coming from the direction of the ice house door, which is about 25 yards from the house. Half his form was soon lifted above the shed. He had probably stepped on an old goods box which was by the side of the shed. She immediately reported to the three men then on guard in the house. One of them stationed himself at the back window. Before the ladies left his guard, footsteps were heard on the shed — the scraping of matches was also heard, and a light seen on the shed. The lady went back to the closet window — the man on the shed had been alarmed and had disappeared. In a few minutes, however, he appeared again, and Mr. Moon's sister-in-law again reported his presence to the guard at the back passage window. She went back immediately to the closet window to look out, she saw a man crouched close to the wall between the two windows — a scraping of matches was heard — a light flashed in at both windows, and the man on the shed rushing by the closet window on the roof of Mr. Moon's chamber, fired a pistol at her, barely missing her head, and singeing her eyebrows, and hair. The powder blackened the side of the house next to the window, and the ball struck and glanced off. The man ran over Mr. Moon's chamber, and jumping down on the other side, escaped.

"Since this last described night, several weeks have elapsed, but no night has passed in which the burglars did not demonstrate their presence, unmistakably in some way or other. Lights have been thrown in at Mr. Moon's windows every night, and frequently over the heads of from 10 to 40 armed men. Sometimes a small light, no larger than a quarter of a dollar is played upon the walls of his houses — sometimes a much larger spot — than a broad or narrow streak — sometimes a flash, and sometimes a broad glare. A bright, radiating light has been seen on the shed at the chamber window, and at the office window.

"The men who watched in Mr. Moon's parlor last night, say that light was thrown in there, they suppose, at least 50 times, apparently an effort was made to throw the shadow of men on the walls. Nearly every night knocking or scraping sounds have been heard on the sides of the house. Stones have been thrown on top or against the house. Footsteps have been heard on the shed and chamber roofs — windows have been opened, or attempts made to open them, or something of the sort has occurred.

"One morning, a roll of cloth about six inches long, and an inch in diameter, saturated with kerosene oil, and burnt at one end, evidently a wick for a large light, was found on top of Mr. Moon's shed. On another morning, a bottle was found in the flower border, covered with two folds of flannel, and having a leather string for a loop to hold it by. The fragments of a broken glass vessel, probably about the size of an orange, have been found on the top of the shed.

"We should add that in the last several weeks, the burglars have been seen five or six times and shot at twice. The demonstrations last night were violent and daring."

And so it went, night after night, the absurdities and terrors continuing with increasing variety and veracity. One night some bricks and rocks that children had piled up, were lugged by the phantom to the roof of the house. On another occasion, a "figure" sailed china plates off the roof. A brick hurled at a nurse rocking an infant grazed the baby's hand.

Four weary neighbors, armed with muskets, sat up most of the night one evening, when toward dawn, with all quiet around the house, they laid down on the parlor carpet and went to sleep. As they did, someone, or something, tiptoed his (or her) way across them to a table in the far corner, removed a heavy music box and family Bible, took off a linen table cover, replaced the objects and dumped the cover by the door, which was slammed. Jerking awake at the sudden noise, the four men saw "lights playing on the door," but no sign of the prowling prankster.

Mrs. Butts, Moon's niece, adds more manifestations to the account, which occurred after the Scottsville Register article appeared. She told of the experiences of their uncle's butler at the house. "He said the bed of my uncle's beautiful young daughter used to rise up to the ceiling when the ghost came near. The butler said the ghost left the silver and other valuables untouched, but would always drink up the whiskey and brandy from my uncle's decanters; and that once he actually consumed a demijohn known to have been full at bedtime.

Mrs. Butts continued: "One night the butler returned late and left his groceries on the dining room table. The ghost emptied everything together, coffee, sugar, flour, meal, salt and soda, and then poured New Orleans molasses over the mixture. Gathering up the four corners of the cloth, he deposited his 'witches brew' and a family Bible on the roof, a favorite spot with him.

"It was from the shed roof that he fired a shot which singed the hair and eyebrow of my uncle's sister-in-law, Miss Kate Tompkins, and at other times hurled rocks and dinner plates through the air. Able to aim close without inflicting injury, the ghost was equally adept at escaping bullets.

"Although the ghost made many peculiar noises, the only complete sentence ever heard from him was: 'Surround the house, boys!' spoken when he and a number of his confederates rushed madly toward the house, masked and clad in overcoats and Confederate capes. They were off again before the watchers had time to shoot. The ghost apparently wore armor, for chains were heard to rattle at times, especially when he raced around the cottage, shaking windows and doors as he went, one night toward the last when he appeared, tall and white, on the front porch. Shot at, the clank of chains was heard when he fell, but he was up and off before the watchers could reach the porch. They found a puddle of blood where he fell. Some claim this 'blood' was pokeberry juice; others say an examination at the University of Virginia showed it to be either ox blood or human blood.

"The butler said that late that night four men were ferried across the river at Scottsville, carrying something which looked like a litter with a covered body on it. He also said that thereafter one of his old colored friends had been 'so pestered by the ghost of the ghost' that he was forced to move back and forth across James River every six weeks to keep the ghost away, because 'it takes a ghost six weeks to cross water.'"

Finally in the summer of 1868, the ghost or person ceased his nocturnal activities at the Moon House. He left his "visiting card" in the form of a note tied to a long reed. Mrs. Butts said, "when my uncle opened the front door, pistol in hand, in response to some pebbles thrown against the door, the reed fell into the hall . . . It was written in pencil on cheap paper with a zig-zag scroll drawn around these words: 'Master Jack . . . I will not pester you eny more . . . Jack Ghost."

There were no more manifestations at Moon House.

Was the Moon ghost a ghost? Or was he a persistent prankster seeking revenge for some real or perceived past slight? A case could be made either way. Whoever heard of a ghost writing a note . . . . or even more implausibly, firing a gun? Still, if it wasn't a ghost, how would one explain the Houdini-like escapes which continued, sometimes nightly, for two years? Surely, in all that time, with all the hundreds of guards and witnesses who kept watch at the Moon house from 1866 to 1868 — somewhere, somehow, someone would have seen or run into someone mortal. And so it remains — to this day — one of the great unsolved mysteries of the Commonwealth of Virginia.

There is even a surreal footnote to this absorbing saga. In her talk to the Albemarle Historical Society, Frances Moon Butts said that she had received many letters from people all over the world regarding her uncle's famous ghost. One came from a woman in Pennsylvania who said that there was a spirit which appeared every 50 years at the "old Moon stronghold" in England.

Her curiosity piqued, Mrs. Butts did some extensive research, and traced the Virginia Moons back to Dunster Castle in the "Lorna Doone" country of England. "In 1933," she said, "I visited Dunster Castle. Built on a 'tor' or small mountain, as is Monticello, it overlooks the southern shores of the Bristol Channel and dates back to an original grant from William the Conqueror.

"A young man guided me through the old entrance gate, around a wall ten-feet thick at places, until finally we left the winding road to continue our ascent up a long flight of foot-worn stone steps through a darkly wooded section. I was wondering about the ghost but dared not ask, for fear of hearing a story 'built to please,' but when suddenly the guide turned and said: 'They call this Jacob's Ladder, because the ghost walks here.' I replied as innocently as possible: 'Do you have a ghost at Dunster Castle?' He answered: 'Yes, every 50 years. His last visit was in 1916, and the people who were living down in Dunster Town at the time say they used to hear him moan and scream up and down this path.

"Nineteen-sixteen was exactly 50 years from 1866!"

C H A P T E R   1 3

The Case of the Haunted Castle

ne of the more colorful, but little-remembered Virginia colonists of note was a merchant named Francis Jerdone, born in Jedbury, Scotland, who emigrated to America in 1746. He arrived at Yorktown and opened a store "which met with unusual success." It was written that, "Mr. Jerdone has a very busy store." Visiting warehouses along the York, Pamunkey and Mattapony Rivers, and gaining friends and customers among the planters, he prospered in the tobacco business.

In 1752, Jerdone bought a tract of land containing 1,000 acres lying between Plum Tree Branch and Great Rockey Creek along the North Anna River, and soon after, he built a house there which came to be known as Jerdone's Castle. It still stands today. It is early colonial with a basement, a story and a half, large end chimneys and dormer windows. A little more than a century later, General Clayton C. Coleman, who married Jerdone's granddaughter, built a huge addition which virtually dwarfs the original house.

This newer part has four rooms each in the basement, and on the first and second floors, and to say these rooms are spacious is an understatement. They are 20 feet by 20 feet, with center halls, running 14 feet by 40. There are abundant large fireplaces and beautiful mantels and woodwork.

There also is an almost sinister atmosphere about the place. One former resident called the castle a "really eerie" house. She said there were all sorts of turrets, and winding spiral staircases "full of spider webs. They really give you the creeps, especially in the dark." Others have said the old root cellar gives the appearance of having been a dungeon.

Before moving into his new castle, in the middle of the 18th century, Francis Jerdone lived in Providence Forge and established a store there. He did well here, too, and eventually bought the town's forge, bakery, and other milling manufactures, plus a large number of slaves. When he died in 1771, Jerdone had extensive business operations in York, Louisa, and Albemarle counties as well as Providence Forge. It is said he died a rich man.

Sometime before his death, the wily old Scotsman told his family that a "substantial portion" of his wealth was in bars and wedges of gold, and when he was laid to rest, his sons and daughters felt that the lion's share of this horde was missing and must have been hidden somewhere in the house, or buried on the grounds. There is evidence that a lot of digging went on under the house and in the surrounding area, but nothing was ever found.

There even were reports that vandals had dug holes all through the small family cemetery which lies close by, but current castle owner Jack Deaton laughs at those suggestions. "Oh, there were a lot of holes running between the tombstones in the cemetery," he says, "but they were made by groundhogs."

And, aside from the legends of buried gold, there also are tales of a ghost or ghosts still showing up at Jerdone's Castle. "We've heard of such stories ever since we bought the property about 30 years ago," Deaton says. "One person who lived here sometime ago, said her grandparents told her that when they were here — back in the days before the automobile — they often would see lights heading down the road towards them at night, getting larger and brighter as they approached. And then they would mysteriously disappear before reaching the house."

"There is supposed to be a ghost here," says Mrs. Deaton. "We heard it was Sara, Francis Jerdone's wife. Why she would come back, I don't know." Jack Deaton adds that one former resident said she once saw "somebody in a white dress one night" in the house when no one was there.

An interesting sidelight is the fact that famous Virginia novelist Ellen Glasgow lived at Jerdone's castle from 1879 to 1888. Her house on Main Street in Richmond has long been thought to be haunted by the return of her spirit. George Washington also spent a night at the castle in 1791.

"I don't put a whole lot of stock in the stories about ghosts," Deaton says. "Maybe that's because I don't necessarily believe in such things. But I will have to say that there is one occurrence that has taken place a number of times over the years and I have never been able to explain it. We have a wardrobe in one of the big rooms on the right, and 'she,' Miss Sara, that is, opens it up sometimes. I mean the wardrobe opens without any visible force. I suppose it could be something like a shift in the weight on the floor, but I doubt that. I don't know what causes it."

Deaton did say that one woman tenant at the house was certain it was haunted. "She was sure there was something there," he remembers. "She never saw anything, just said there was like a presence around. She sensed something. I will say that one day she was grilling on a barbecue out back on the patio, and all of a sudden the fire leaped out of the grill and was burning on the ground. There was no wind to speak of, and I couldn't tell you how it happened, or why. She swore it was the ghost, and it convinced her. She promptly moved out of the house after only being there a month."

CHAPTER 14

Mystery Footprints at Oakland Farm

hen Mrs. Margaret Shepherd was a principal at a school in Palmyra in Fluvanna County in the 1920s, she often drove by the old house on her way to work without noticing it. It was set back from the road not far from Boyd Tavern beneath several towering oaks. One day she did notice Oakland Farm. In fact, she says she felt somehow "drawn" to it. She looked at it for a long time and said she "had a very definite feeling that this was my house, my home."

Whether or not Mrs. Shepherd had psychic abilities is not known, but at least in this case, her instincts were dead right. As it turned out, she fell in love with a man a few months later, and on their wedding day he took her to Oakland and told her his grandmother had owned it and had given it to them as a wedding gift! She was, in a word, astonished. And then, when he took her on a tour inside, she said she knew, without being shown or told, where every door led to. She couldn't explain why, she just knew. "I can remember when my husband pointed to a closed door and told me he couldn't recall where that went to, and I said 'why it goes down to a basement room'," Mrs. Shepherd said years later. and when they opened the door and went down the stairs, there was a brick walled room there just as she had somehow known it would be.

The room that fascinated her the most, however, was a small seldom-used parlor on the first floor. There was a framed picture of a little girl of about six or seven over the mantel. The girl was dead. The young face was described as "lovely," and the girl had long hair that had been carefully brushed. Mrs. Shepherd said the picture intrigued her and she seemed to develop a "strong sense of identity" with the girl. For a long time afterward, she said, she dreamed about her.

Soon after the Shepherds moved in, the multiple manifestations began. The newly-wed couple heard sleigh bells, but saw no sleighs. Mrs. Shepherd would often hear the sounds of music and conversation in the house, when she knew she was there alone. In one interview, she told the writer, "It was like being in a hotel when a big party was being held in the ballroom. Many times I hear 'them' on New Year's Eve when my husband and I happened to be celebrating here alone. One New Year's Eve we drank champagne here in this room at midnight. The laughter and music were very plain. I said, 'Well, they're really whooping it up tonight'."

There were other sounds. One night Mrs. Shepherd was startled awake in the middle of the night by the sound of a "tremendous crash." She said it was as if someone had opened the front door and then slammed it as hard as they could against the wall. This was followed by "heavy footsteps" crossing the floor. She went downstairs to investigate, but found nothing amiss.

Although the occurrences continued for several decades at Oakland Farm, Mrs. Shepherd says she was frightened only once. "I always felt that if there were ghosts in the house, they were friendly and liked having me there," she once said. The only occasion when she felt fear, took place one day when she was sewing in the second floor bedroom. Steps led to the attic from this room. Suddenly, she heard footsteps — "heavy and deliberate" — come down the attic stairs and stop at the bedroom door. She later told Charlottesville author Naomi Hintz that she was "paralyzed with fright" as she stared at the closed door. She said there was no doubt in her mind that an "intruder" had hidden in the attic and was waiting until she was alone in the house. "Now, of course," she told Hintze, "anyone with any sense would have run down the stairs and out of the house, but I went and opened that door. Nobody was there. I searched the attic and found no signs that anyone had been there."

Others who stayed as guests in that room told her they, too, had heard the footsteps, sometimes right up to the edge of their bed, but nothing was ever seen.

Solid evidence of supernatural happenings developed one winter when an electrician came to Oakland Farm to install a light switch on the wall inside the attic stairs. He left a thick coating of plaster dust on the stairs. Soon after, the housekeeper, a Mrs. Clement, found white footprints on the bare waxed floor. They led into the room and then back toward the attic door. At first, Mrs. Clement, annoyed, assumed that the electrician had carelessly walked about in the mess, but on close examination it was noticed that the prints were

of *bare* feet! They were immense, at least size 12 or larger, and the imprint of the toes was spread out as if the person who made them had never worn shoes.

Mrs. Clement cleaned the room, but the tracks reappeared two weeks later, and this time there were two sets: one was the return of "big foot," and the other was a set of very small prints, like those of a child. Mrs. Clement cleaned up all the plaster dust in the room and on the attic stairs, and the footprints were not seen again until the following spring, when tracks were made in pollen dust. The prints reoccurred in later years when the pollen was in the air, but Mrs. Shepherd could not find a rational reason for the prints, and it remained a mystery until one year Dr. William Roll, then the project director of the Psychical Research Foundation in Durham, North Carolina, and Douglas Johnson, a well-known British medium, visited the house. They came after Naomi Hintze and Dr. J. Gaither Pratt, a parapsychologist at the University of Virginia, had visited Oakland Farms and interviewed Mrs. Shepherd for their subsequent book, "The Psychic Realm: What Can You Believe," and suggested that Dr. Roll and Johnson investigate the house for themselves.

Johnson offered a solution to the origins of the mysterious footprints. He believed the small ones to be that of a little girl, and the gigantic ones to be that of a huge Negro woman, who probably had served as mammy to the girl in years long gone by. He also envisioned the little girl as dying of a "choking sickness." This was, he said, a very sad time in the house. Mrs. Shepherd said that there had been a long-held tradition there that a greatly bereaved father at Oakland had refused to bury his seven-year-old daughter who had died of diphtheria. One night while he slept, a black servant and the family doctor took the girl from the house and buried her.

Whether or not this fits in with another vision that the psychic Johnson had during his visit is not known, but it possibly could be related. He said he saw and heard the sounds of women sobbing, and, as he looked through a window, he saw several men in black walking down over the lawn to the place where there once was an old icehouse, partly below ground. Johnson said the men went down the steps into the icehouse (which did not even exist at the time he envisioned this) and they came up "bearing a coffin."

In her later years, Mrs. Shepherd opened a school for children with learning disabilities at Oakland Farm. But even with all these active people — students and counselors — around, the ghostly manifestations continued, although they took different forms. Several people, for example reported sightings of "glowing, orange balls" in the area. One young man spotted such an object in the woods in back of the school. He said it was about 25 feet above the ground, and he watched it descend to the ground, getting smaller as it went, and finally disappearing. He ran back into a building shouting, "this place is haunted!"

Another counselor sighted an oblong shape he said was about two feet long and very bright. He said it hovered over some unmarked graves on the grounds. When he went inside to get others to come out and witness the phenomena, it had vanished. Still another young man at the school saw a mysterious "white glow" in the rear view mirror of his car one night as he was driving on the property. He said the glow seemed to be following his car, and he had the sensation of intense cold. He said he could barely breathe. Then, the flowing light swept around to the side and then the front of his car. Terrified, he turned the car around and headed back to get his roommate. But by the time he roused him, the eerie light was gone.

And then there was the death and the return of a nameless 12 year old student, who was described as having "a Roman nose and a Julius Caesar haircut." He was also very large for his age, and awkward. But the counselors more or less adopted him during the school year and looked forward to his return following vacation period. He never came back, however. Word came to the school that he had drowned at Virginia Beach.

Then one night a counselor saw him. It was, he said, a dark

windy night with strange cloud formations in the sky. In a clearing, a few feet in front of him, the counselor saw him. A tall, looming figure with a Roman nose and a Julius Caesar haircut. The witness said he was positive it wasn't a "flesh and blood" person, although he couldn't see through the person. He was convinced it was the likeable young boy who had drowned the previous summer.

Mrs. Shepherd said she never could find a rational explanation for all the strange happenings over the years at Oakland Farm. In his book, "The Psychic Realm," Dr. Pratt noted, "the sincerity of Mrs. Shepherd is beyond question, so I have no reason to doubt that she is representing the facts as she remembers them." The parapsychologist seemed particularly interested in the footprints in the plaster dust and the pollen made by "phantom feet," because most ghost investigators agree that spirits do not leave tangible evidence of their presence.

So even Dr. Pratt could not explain the ethereal events that have occurred at Oakland Farm.

CHAPTER 15

The Psychic Proffitts of Lovingston

(Author's note: After writing four previous regional Virginia ghost books (Williamsburg, Richmond, Tidewater, and Fredericksburg), it should come as no surprise that I get a considerable amount of mail during the year from people who have had psychic experiences and want to share them. Some have called or written and said they had previously been afraid to speak about ghostly occurrences for fear that people would think them crazy. From the always-interesting correspondence, I have, through he years, gleaned some entertaining stories for inclusion in this series of books.

Such was the case a year or so ago when a young lady named Nancy Connor sent a check for a copy of one of my books, and enclosed a succinct, yet intriguing note. It said, simply, "My mother lived in the Proffitt House in Lovingston. 'Helen" still lives there." I was hooked. I tracked Nancy down to her home in Tampa, Florida, and she led me onto a number of other sources who, like her, contributed to the following, and I think fascinating, chapter.)

an an entire family clan be psychic? There are cases on file where the psychic "gift" apparently has been handed down from parent to child, sometimes covering centuries. In other instances those "born to see" may skip a generation or two. The Proffitts of Lovingston — the town about halfway between Charlottesville and Lynchburg on Route 29 — must surely fit somewhere in one of these categories, because several members of the family have been either on the "giving" or the "receiving" end of spectral manifestations over a lengthy period dating back to the earliest days of the 20th century and perhaps beyond.

The Proffitts are virtually as prominent and as prolific in the area as are the Lovings — the family from which Lovingston took its name. In fact, there still is a Proffitt House on Main Street — a large, three-story structure that likely was built sometime between 1810 and 1815, say Michael and Kay Crabill, the present owners. "Some people believe the house was first constructed in the late 1700s and was a tavern," Kay says, "but all our research indicates that it probably was built shortly after the auction." The is a reference to an event the Lovings staged in 1809. To build up the town they auctioned off parcels of land at dirt-cheap prices to anyone who promised to put up at least a 12 foot by 12 foot structure on the property within three years.

"Some people have told us the ground floor part of the house was constructed first, but we believe the house was all built at one time," Kay says. "The ground floor has a cook-in fireplace and then there are two upper floors. There are only two bedrooms on the third floor, but they are huge rooms, as was the custom at the time it was planned." There also is a wrap-around porch, which runs around three quarters of the house.

"My father bought the house from Grafton Tucker, I think sometime in the 1920s," says Mary Proffitt Walker, now (1992) a still spry and lucid 85-years-old and living in Port Charlotte, Florida. "We lived there for years and years." Mrs. Walker tells of the time, after she had married and moved to Washington, D.C., when a boarder in her house there told of seeing a gentleman in her room standing at the

Mountain Cove Cemetery, near Lovingston

foot of her bed. Then the woman noticed a photograph of Mrs. Walker's father, which had just been reframed, and declared that was the man she saw in her room — John Fletcher Proffitt. Mrs. Walker told her boarder that her father was dead, but that when he had visited her in Washington he always stayed in that same bedroom.

Mary Walker's father and her mother, Verdie Teresa Tyree Proffitt, who lived on a farm at "the Cove," were said to have had a number of scary psychic encounters in and around Mountain Cove church and cemetery. Mrs. Walker and her sister, Estelle Stevens, who stills lives adjacent to the church, both say that their mother was a great story-teller and sometimes told some pretty wild tales.

"But she swore they were true," Mrs. Walker says. "It was quite a colorful era," adds Nancy Connor, Mrs. Walker's daughter. "There was a hanging tree, and my grandfather was involved with the Klu Klux Klan." According to Mrs. Walker and Mrs. Stevens, their parents met up with all sorts of haunts near the church and cemetery, always late at night.

"I can remember my mother telling me that once she and my father were coming from the Cove to Lovingston in a one-horse buggy, carrying a load of fresh eggs to sell to merchants," Mrs. Walker recalls. "As they passed the graveyard, something spooked the horse and it reared up, the buckboard turned over, and all the eggs were broken.

"Another time my mother said they were passing by in the same area when a man ran out of the cemetery with a white sheet over his face. He grabbed the reins and said 'you're not going anywhere.' She said it scared both of them, but that right before their eyes, the man vanished." Mrs. Stevens says still another time, as they were stopped once again passing the churchyard, a man jumped out in front of them with a shawl over his head. He appeared in the shadows to be "Uncle Riley Proffitt" — a member of the family who had been killed in World War I!

Nancy Connor vividly remembers Verdie Proffitt, her grandmother, telling her about one time when Verdie and her husband were passing by Mountain Cove and their horse stopped dead in ins tracks and refused to move. "She said John finally got out of the buggy and put a blanket over the eyes of the horse. Only then, would it start up. Something had shaken it to the marrow," Nancy says. "Grandmother then said, that as they got a few yards away, they both turned back to look, and they saw a headless horseman! She said she was not making up a story, that it actually happened. It should be noted that a number of old timers in the Mountain Cove area have also attested that they have witnessed strange apparitions in and around the church grounds.

Arthur Stevens, Estelle's husband, has heard the stories, too. He grew up in the area and his relatives are dotted throughout the valley community. His ancestors have lived here since the mid-1700s. "I never saw a ghost myself," he says. "I did hear some strange moaning one night by the cemetery, and it gave me a creepy feeling. A lot of slaves are buried there, too, though their graves are unmarked. They used to just put a plain stone on them, but most of them are long gone. Well, the moaning turned out to be a crow sitting up in a tree.

"One time when I was a young man, I came by that old cemetery after I had had a lot to drink. I decided to rest a little, so I laid down in a sunken grave. I wondered later what might have happened if someone had come along and I raised up out of that grave," Arthur laughs. "I reckon they would have thought they had seen a spirit all right!"

Estelle Stevens has had a series of separate ghostly visitations herself in more recent years. She was married earlier to William Byrd and they lived in Roseland, south of Lovingston in the Piney River area. William, allegedly, was a carouser who liked to go out at night looking for action at the nearest watering hole. Estelle sometimes would go out looking for him.

One night William got into a scrape over a woman in some tavern, and he and another man got into a fight that resulted in the man shooting and killing William. There was a lot of conflicting testimony at the subsequent trial, and the man pleaded self defense and got off.

It wasn't long afterwards that William began to return, in spirit form, to visit Estelle. "I would wake up to see him either at the foot of my bed or sitting where he always sat in the room, over in the corner in a chair by the stove," Estelle says. "I would always ask him how he got in the house, and he would say, 'just like I always did,' through the window. Many times I would get up out of bed and walk over to where he was sitting and try to touch him, but whenever I did, he just vanished. He wasn't frightening or anything, but I really didn't know what to do. I wondered if I was going crazy or something. So I finally went to my minister and I told him about William's visits and I asked him what to do. The minister said to tell William that everything was okay, and that I didn't need him anymore and he could go on to where he was supposed to go. So I did that the next time he came into the house, and I never saw him or

heard from him again."

Of all the associations of the Proffitts with psychic phenomena in the area, however, undoubtedly the most tragic involved a four-year-old girl named Helen Loving. She was the daughter of Dora Proffitt Loving, and they lived in the Proffitt House. At the time there were some boarders who lived there also. They packed peaches in the county.

One day in September 1932, little Helen, found some matches in the boarders' room and crawled under the bed and started striking them. Her dress caught fire, and in her terror, Helen ran down the stairs, screaming and then ran outside, running all around the wrap-around porch. The flames spread quickly and by the time others reached her, she had been burned so badly that she died some days later in a Lynchburg hospital.

"Oh, she was something special," says Mrs. Walker. "She was so bright and so pleasant, just a joy to be around. We all loved her so much. Everyone in Lovingston loved the ground that child walked on. We just knew something was going to happen to her."

Fifty years later, Maureen and Joe Boles were living in Proffitt House. "It was a total derelict when we bought it," remembers Maureen, now living in St. Augustine, Florida. "Of course, at the time, we didn't know anything about the house or its past history, or the fact that Helen Loving had been burned there and subsequently died.

"Well, there were a couple of things that we couldn't explain. We had a couple of guests once and they stayed in one of the upstairs bedrooms. They said they had heard a child playing in the room that night, in the corner of the room. They got up, but they couldn't see anything. They said they couldn't stay there anymore, and they left the house.

"There were plenty of other times when you felt like there was sort of a 'presence' in the house. I mean you wouldn't directly see or feel anything, but you still felt kind of uneasy. I can't really explain it, but maybe you know what I mean," Maureen continues.

"And then one day I was down at the base of the stairs when our dog stiffened and began barking. I had a funny feeling. Something told me to look up, and when I did I saw a little girl. She must have been about four years old. My impression is that she was in a long gown, like a night gown. It was an old one, and she looked like she was standing over the steps on her tiptoes and peeping over the bannister at me. She was only there for a second. It was a fleeting glance, but there was no mistaking that she was a little girl. And then she vanished. I checked upstairs, but there was no one there. I never saw her again, just that once."

(Author's note: The description Maureen Boles gave of the little girl she saw matched Helen Loving perfectly. Yet, strangely, Maureen did not know who the girl was, until I informed her of the tragic fire incident during an interview with her in January 1992. Present owners Michael and Kay Crabill say they have not been visited by Helen during their time in the house. They theorize that the little girl must be satisfied that Proffitt House is being well taken care of.)

A Headless Horseman Rides Again

he next time you have a pleasant Saturday or Sunday afternoon (or any day for that matter, depending upon your schedule) on your hands, you might try driving down toward Lynchburg from Charlottesville on Route 29. About five miles north of the town of Amherst, south of Lovingston, you will see a small road sign bearing a cluster of grapes that says "tours." Turn right at the dirt road, go back a short way, and you will be at the Rebec winery. It is small as Virginia vineyards go, only about four acres of grapes, but owner-operator Richard Hanson proudly will match his quality with the best in the state. And, indeed, his classic, oakey chardonnays, and his robust cabernet sauvignons, along with several table wines, would well justify such a sidetrip in themselves, especially in the spring, summer, or fall when one can picnic on the adjacent hillside amidst a splendorous backdrop of mountains.

But there is more. As one approaches the winery, off to the right, flanked by antique dependency buildings, is a rustic, 250-year-old house — called Mountain View. And, as you probably guessed by now, Mountain View is haunted. "Oh, yes, we have our resident ghost," says a spry, articulate and delightful Ella Hanson, the 80-year-young wife of Richard. "He might scare you a little as he did me the first time I experienced his presence, but he means no harm," she laughs.

The house, Ella will tell you, was built in 1742 on Spencer's Mountain. It was moved to its present location sometime around 1830. "They moved everything but the cellar. They left that up on the mountain," Ella says. "It was in the Cabell family for a long time, and my grandparents bought it in 1877. This house has personality. It has

feelings. You can feel people here. But it's not scary. Guests have told me that they can sense the house has 'really been lived in.'

While Richard remains a skeptic, Ella believes she and some of her ancestors may be sensitive to psychic phenomena. "Take my great-grandmother Goode, for example. During the battle of Mount Jackson in the Civil War she had a vision that one of her sons had his horse shot out from under him and he was killed. She wrote to the boy's uncle and told him to bring her son home — before anyone officially informed her of his death. As it turned out, he died exactly as she had envisioned!"

Ella herself once had a similar experience when she was a young girl of 12 or 13; that would put it about 1924 or 1925. "My father was out working on the railroad at the time," she recalls. "And I was in the kitchen. I was in what we called a 'brown study.' That is, there was absolutely nothing on my mind. I wasn't thinking about anything. That's the time when you sometimes get psychic impressions. Anyway, I looked up and saw my father come into the kitchen. He was smiling and swinging his lunchbox. I wondered what was he doing home at this time of day. And then I ran up to hug him, *and he wasn't there*! My arms went right through him! I screamed, and when I told my mother about the episode, she chided me and said I had been seized by the devil.

Ella Hanson sits on her grandfather's bed, which she has "shared" with an unseen guest.

"A little while later, we had a telegram delivered to the house. It said my father had been seriously injured in an accident at Sparrow's Point. He lost one leg below the knee and three fingers, and it happened at precisely the instant I saw his apparition come into the kitchen!"

Ella also remembers a ghostly encounter she had when her grandmother was still living. "I guess I was about 16 then and it was after midnight. The night was so still, you could hear the animals outside the house. I had gone upstairs and gotten in my grandmother's bed," she says. "Sometime later, it must have been one or two in the morning, I heard footsteps coming up the stairs, and I assumed it was my grandmother coming up to tell me to get in my own bed, and I jumped up to tell her I was. The door handle turned slowly, and then the door opened. There was no one there. I learned later that grandmother had stayed downstairs."

The most recent phenomenon occurred about five years ago, but remains as fresh as yesterday to Ella. She describes it: "I went to bed, I forget what time it was, but it must have been late at night. We sleep in my great grandparent's bed. Anyway, shortly after I got settled, I felt a nice warm presence get into bed beside me and I, or course, thought it was Richard. So I said 'did you just get in bed with me, Richard?' And Richard called out from the other room that he hadn't. I said, 'yes you did.' And he said no he didn't. But you could feel the mattress give way, as it does when someone lies down on it, and you could literally feel the impression being made in the mattress. You could feel an indentation. I wasn't really scared, but when I told Richard about it, he just laughed and he kidded me a lot.

"Well, some time later, I was doing some work. It must have been somewhere between one and three a.m., and I heard Richard call out, 'Ella, did you just get in the bed?' I said no. The same thing had happened to him. He hasn't mocked me about my ghost since."

* * * * *

Ella Hanson also tells of some fascinating and rich legends involving an old race track that was on one of her ancestor's farms in the Clifford area. It was, she believes from what she can remember and from what grandparents and others told her as a child, about a mile and a quarter around and race horses were brought there from as far away as Kentucky and Baltimore. It is not readily known when the track was built, or when the races began, but Ella says they apparently were run annually up to the days of the Civil War. "My grandmother told me they were really exciting days. The races would last for about 10 days or two weeks, and that everyone would have a good time. She said some of the wagers on the races, proba-

bly after a number of juleps, would be astronomical. One house was won, lost and won again all in one afternoon."

Ella doesn't know exactly when the ghost legend associated with the track was born. It may have happened sometime between 1830 and 1850. "I can remember hearing that there was a great tragedy at the races one day. Apparently, one of the riders had a terrible accident. I have heard that he broke his neck. I have also heard that he was decapitated. I don't know if it was because of a fall, or if he may have run into a tree branch or something.

"What I do know, is that ever since that time, people have periodically reported the sounds of horses, and the apparitional sight of a headless rider chasing them. My grandfather said he was once accosted by this ghostly rider. He was a very honorable man, and he never drank. When he said something, you knew it was the gospel. He said he was coming home one night and as he passed Chewning's place, he could feel some sort of presence. He knew there was another rider behind him. He said he had a terrible time controlling his horse, which was spooked. The phantom horseman followed him all the way to the racetrack farm, and then it suddenly disappeared. Grandfather swore he not only heard the horse's hooves, but he also could hear the animal breathe. He wasn't a man to make up tales."

Ella says there was a number of reports of such sightings as the tradition grew over the years. "It would really terrify some people," she says. We had a black servant working for the family named Grace. She came running into the house in hysterics one evening, shaking so hard we had to give her a sedative. She was white as a sheet! When she finally calmed down some, she said she had been followed by a man without a head on a horse.

"Many people, too, have reported hearing 'racetrack' sounds years after the track was closed. My grandmother said she can recall as a child lying down in an upstairs bedroom, and on days when the wind was blowing a certain way, she could distinctly hear a number of horses' hooves roar past the house, and the voices of men shouting 'Hi, ya, hi, ya.' Others have reported hearing similar sounds."

. . . And so, if you have the time some lazy afternoon, drive on down to the Rebec winery just north of Amherst. You can sip some fine wine, enjoy the mountain scenery, and, just possibly, if the conditions are right, you might close your eyes and hear the far off sounds of ghostly thoroughbreds racing around a track 150 years in the past!

The Ill Fated Insurrection
at Islington

If ever anyone had just cause to come back from the great beyond seeking vengeance for their violent death on earth, such a person might be General Terisha Washington Dillard, a rich plantation owner along the James River in Amherst County in the middle of the 1800s. Dillard owned an estate called Islington, located between Stapleton and Riverville. His property also included an island in the James.

In the fateful year of 1863, as General Robert E. Lee and his courageous and faithful "lieutenants" traded body blows with Union forces throughout the Commonwealth, Dillard had managed to hold onto about 20 slaves, most of them children. His holdings were valued at about $40,000 — a princely sum at the time. He was considered a wealthy land baron and owned other properties in Amherst as well as Fluvanna County.

Apparently, one of his more recently acquired slaves was from Louisiana; a strong young man with a rebellious streak. Sensing that freedom was near, this slave convinced the others that they could hasten their liberty by overtaking Dillard and stealing his money. Just how this bloody coup came to be was recounted in the mid 1970s in a series of articles by Meg Hibbert in the Amherst New Era-Progress on Amherst County houses and the tales told about them. The article quoted Mrs. J. B. Stovall (Queena Dillard Stovall) of Elon. Terisha Washington Dillard was her great uncle, and Mrs. Stovall had been told the story by her mother.

"A woman slave murdered Uncle Terry as part of a plot by the slaves to get his property and money," Mrs. Stovall related. "The woman who murdered him was supposed to have been influenced by a new slave from Louisiana who had ideas of insurrection. This was during the Civil War, you know.

"Mother told me Uncle Terry was upstairs in one of the out-buildings — Islington was still in the process of being built. He was counting his eggs, and looked out the window to see the Negroes out in the yard planning something. He could see them whispering and watching for him," Mrs. Stovall continued.

"They went after him. He didn't have anything to defend himself with, but he fought his way down the steps of the little house. When he got to the bottom, there was a Negro woman who hit him in the head with an axe. (Other accounts of this gruesome incident state that Dillard's head was cut off.) The slaves took him out and buried him in the hog lot. It was several days before people knew what had happened to him.

"The way it was found out was that Grandpa saw some of the young men playing mumble peg, and saw that one had Uncle Terry's pocket knife. People investigated and found out which slave had killed him and where the body was buried."

It is likely that at the time, considering the brazen brutality of the murder, a lynching might have been seriously considered, but Mrs. Stovall's mother said a regular trial was held and that 11 Negroes eventually were hanged. The young woman who had struck the fatal axe blow was pregnant at the time, and the authorities waited until after she delivered a baby boy, and then they hanged her.

Mary E. Dillard, Terry's widow, completed the house after her husband's death and the property remained in the family until early in the 20th century. Colonel Soren Listoe, a consul to Belgium during the first World War, bought Islington in 1912 and then sold it back to the Dillards in 1925. Whether or not his selling of the estate had anything to do with the alleged return of Terry Dillard's ghost is not known, but acquaintances said Colonel Listoe "could never account for strange noises" at the house. Through the years others have reported psychic experiences on the grounds which led them to conclude that "Dillard's spirit still lingers around the area." When Tom Larkin, Dillard's grandson, inherited the property in 1963, he admitted that people told him the house was haunted.

On the night following Halloween in 1969, four area juveniles set fire to the old brick mansion. All that is left today is a portion of the brick walls, the ancient boxwoods, and the lasting legend that those who are adventurous enough to walk about the ruins late on moonlit evenings may catch a glimpse of a shadowy figure stealthily stalking about. The figure is, it is said, either seeking retribution for a cruel crime endured long ago, or, as some said, it is searching for its severed head!

CHAPTER 1 8

Sarah Henry's Return to Winton

(Author's personal note: I am delighted to recount the following story about a very famous ghost who haunts a historic mansion which is now part of the Winton Country Club in Clifford, a tiny crossroads in Amherst County about two-thirds of the way from Charlottesville towards Lynchburg. My paternal ancestors are from this area and I was born in Lynchburg. Each summer for the past several years I have played in the annual member-guest golf tournament at Winton with my dear cousin, Floyd Layton Taylor, who runs a country store near Monroe just off Route 29. The annual highlight is a dinner and dance held in the Winton mansion.

In the summer of 1985, I was captivated by a tour of the great house conducted by Frank E. Hodgkins, then manager of the club. In one of the large front rooms, over a brandy, Frank told me about the psychic encounters he had experienced there while he lived in residence. They occurred often over a period of a few years. My journalistic instincts told me to take notes, although I had no plans to write about the area at that time. I'm glad I did, because Frank is gone, and the notes were a great help in refreshing my memory.)

here is no reference in any of the multiple biographies about that great Virginian and American statesman Patrick Henry to indicate that he was psychic in any way, or that he ever experienced any unusual phenomena during his long and illustrious career. Yet, curiously, there are at least two noteworthy accounts of ghostly manifestations involving members of his immediate family. One concerned his first wife, Sarah who allegedly was tormented mentally, died relatively young, and comes back infrequently in spirit form at the grand house,

Scotchtown, near Ashland, where Patrick Henry lived in the 1770s. (This was published in the book, "The Ghosts of Fredericksburg and Nearby Environs.")

The second haunting — the one at Winton — concerns the periodic "return" of Sarah Winston Syme Henry, Patrick Henry's mother. Her ancestors emigrated from Wales to the Colony of Virginia, and it has been said that the Winstons were distantly related to the Duke of Marlborough. Sarah became a widow in 1731 when her first husband, Colonel John Syme, died, leaving her a large plantation.

William Byrd II, upon meeting Mrs. Henry in October 1732, wrote the following description in one of his diaries: "The lady, at first suspecting I was some lover, put on a gravity which becomes a weed, but as soon as she learned who I was, brightened up into an unusual cheerfulness and serenity. She was a portly, handsome dame . . . and seemed not to pine too much for the death of her husband." Byrd found Sarah a woman of lively and cheerful conversation, and he noted that she was much less reserved than most of her countrywomen — a trait which set off her other agreeable qualities to advantage.

Sarah soon was remarried to a young Scotsman named John Henry and they had two sons and seven daughters. Patrick Henry was born May 29, 1736. Historians contend that great men on the

whole seem to have been influenced more by their mothers than by their fathers. Whether or not this was true of Patrick, his mother was, say biographers, a woman of superior qualities, with an abiding influence on her famous son. She also was known to have "remarkable intellectual gifts," and an "unusual command of language," which may help explain how Patrick became such a splendid orator. It also has been documented that Thomas Jefferson, on his way to his retreat at Poplar Forest from Monticello, made a point of stopping off to see her. Further, it is recorded that her famous son often sought her out in times of stress.

Sarah Henry came to live at Winton either in 1779 or the early 1780s. The late Georgian house had been built in the 1770s for Joseph Cabell, who served with distinction as an officer in the Revolutionary War. Cabell sold Winton in 1779 to Samuel Meredith, another distinguished military and civic leader who married Patrick Henry's sister. Today, the interior of the structure preserves its early robust woodwork, whose outstanding feature is the drawing room chimneypiece decorated with pilasters and pediment. The woodwork is attributed to the craftsmanship of Hessian prisoners. Early in the 20th century the house was remodeled and portico was added.

One of the colorful legends associated with Winton happened during the Civil War, as Northern troops approached. The lady of the house at the time pulled up some floor planks in the adjoining smokehouse and hastily concealed the family silver and a number of prized hams. When the soldiers arrived, one of her young sons innocently asked them if they were looking for the hams his mother buried. He led them to the spot and they feasted.

Sarah Henry died on Christmas Day 1784. She was placed in a black walnut coffin with quilted silk lining, and a tiny pillow of the choicest goose tender. Patrick Henry, impeded by a heavy snow, could not get to the funeral from Richmond. She was laid to rest in the family burial plot not far from the house, beneath a hand-fashioned brick arch, the length of the grave, made to protect her "against wild animals and wild elements." Her son-in-law, Colonel Samuel Meredith, said at the time, "When I die, lay my body just here, so that for all time I may lie at the feet of the deeply venerated and beloved mother of my wife." His wish was carried out.

There is justifiable cause for Sarah Henry's "return," even though her son-in-law, Colonel Meredith, said at the time of her death, "Her removal to the world of spirits ought by no means to occasion grief to her near and dear connections, as they certainly must rest assured that she is not only received into the Heavenly mansions, but (is) very exalted there." According to family accounts, Colonel Meredith placed, with his own hands, a mound of bricks over Sarah Henry's grave.

However, after Winton passed out of the hands of Sarah's descendants, in 1839, the spot where she was buried was all but forgotten. The bricks which had been placed over her grave became scattered, and the graveyard was overgrown. Many people forgot where Patrick Henry's mother was buried. In fact, 104 years after she had died, Dr. R. A. Brock, secretary of the Virginia Historical Society, wrote that she had been laid to rest at Studley, where she had once lived in Hanover County.

In 1893, Sarah's great granddaughter, Mrs. Edward A. Cabell, at the age of 90, journeyed to Winton to have the small cemetery resurveyed and a plat made. But she failed to arouse any interest in having a "suitable memorial" placed at the site. Nine years later another descendent came to gather the "relics of the shattered tomb and with them, marked the outlines of the grave." Finally, in 1910, other relatives were able to erect a marble tombstone which can be seen today. It says, simply, "Sarah Winston Henry, Mother of Patrick Henry... Died in 1784."

Today the site is fenced in, and a sign placed by the Daughters of the American Revolution signifies the significance of the spot, overlooking the Blue Ridge Mountains.

Just when Sarah Henry's spirit first made its presence known at Winton is uncertain. Years ago, in her book "Houses Virginians Have Loved," author Agnes Rothery wrote that when one visits the house, "her unique personality is immediately felt."

Frank Hodgkins, the former manager of the club at Winton, was more specific during an informal interview in 1985 with the author. "Oh, she has been here for many years," he said. "For how long, I'm not sure, but she made herself known to a number of people before I came here. In fact, I'm told that one of the managers before me had a 'confrontation' with her ghost, fled from the club, and vowed that he would never come back under any circumstances.

"Personally, I heard her footsteps the first night I slept in the house. I was reading in the living room when I heard her in the room above, as if she were pacing about. I went up to look, but there was no one there. At least no one I could see.

"Over the years, I have felt her presence in many ways," Hodgkins said. "She has followed me around at times. Frequently, I heard the swishing of a petticoat. She even touched me on occasions. There was never anything malicious or foreboding about the inci-

dents. It wasn't as if she were trying to scare me. I just think she wanted me to know she was still around, and perhaps seeing if I was keeping the house up to her standards.

"I can tell you of one incident that took place a few years ago (the 1970s). I was scheduled to fly to Boston to accept an award, but I had a premonition that she somehow was trying to warn me not to make the trip. It was a very strong feeling. I canceled the flight, and that plane crashed upon landing in Boston, killing several people. I have no doubt that Sarah Henry saved my life!"

CHAPTER 19

A Legacy of Lynchburg
Legends

* * * * *

THE NAGGING SHREW OF GEDDES

There must be something about the Clifford area of Amherst county which ghosts find appealing. Maybe the country air is conducive to psychic phenomena. It is in this area that Patrick Henry's mother, Sarah, returns from her nearby grave to make her presence known at historic Winton. Down the road a bit is the Rebec winery and the 250-year-old house called Mountain View which also has been visited by a phantom gentleman. And there is the legend of the headless rider who used to be a jockey at a century-and-a-half-old Clifford racetrack.

So it should not be surprising to learn that the discarnate spirit of a nagging wife can still be heard on occasion at Geddes, the ancestral home of the Reverend Robert Rose, also in the singular area. The one-and-a-half-story, white-washed house was built in 1748, and has its own historical anecdotes to share. It served, for example, as a "way station" for Thomas Jefferson and his family during the Revolutionary War. In a letter dated January 11, 1781, Jefferson wrote, "I then rejoined my family at Col. Roses's and proceeded with them to Poplar Forest in Bedford." The future President was referring to his narrow escape in Charlottesville from Colonel Tarleton and his men during a British foray into Albemarle County to capture the colony's legislators.

One of the first houses built in the Clifford area, Geddes has nine rooms with two large rock chimneys near each end which open into huge fireplaces in the cellar. Food was prepared in these fireplaces.

"Geddes was the center of activity when we were growing up in the early 1900s," said Mrs. Jane Claiborne Calkins during an interviewing the mid-1970s. "My parents loved to dance. Here in the parlor is where we used to dance all night. We didn't have electricity then, and we'd sit out dances in the semi-dark on the steps going upstairs. . . .We would have a big supper at midnight, and dance until the crack of dawn."

Mrs. Calkins says it was during these years that she and others heard many strange noises in the house, mostly coming from the cellar. Others have reported hearing the piano being played in the house when no one was inside. The ghost, according to local lore which runs back as far as anyone living can remember, was said to be "Miss Hugh" Rose, wife of Colonel Hugh Rose, son of the builder, Reverend Rose. It was Hugh who added a study onto the west end of the house, which is reachable only from the outside. He did it to escape the constant nagging of his wife.

And so, it is from the study that the piano music can be heard, generally on moonlit nights. Miss Hugh seems still bent on disturbing her husband who often escaped to his retreat in life. "When we were small, every time we'd hear a noise we'd say, 'that must be Miss Hugh,' laughs Mrs. Calkins. Some have even reported seeing the apparitional figure of Miss Hugh riding side saddle through the fields surrounding Geddes. No one has ever sighted the Colonel, but the legend persists that wherever he might be, his sharp-tongued wife is in close pursuit.

* * * * *

THE WORRIED MOTHER

here is a short but rather interesting story concerning the spectral return of a mother concerned about the disturbance of the dead that has been circulating in and around Amherst County for 75 to 100 years or more. The problem is the details, as to exactly where in the county this episode took place, and specifically which family or families it involved, apparently have been lost in the mists of time.

It seems a family bought an old farm and worked it in peace for some time. Then one day, the husband started to plow up a 20-acre lot. His wife, upon returning to the house that day after completing her milking chores, saw a woman dressed in black standing at the basement door. The woman was crying. she also appeared to be in spirit form.

The wife was terrified. She experienced the exact same phenomena for the next three days, and finally told her husband that she couldn't handle it any more. She told him about the apparitional woman and then asked him if they could move. He told her that the next time she saw the mystery woman, if indeed she ever saw her again, to speak to her and find out what she wanted.

Sure enough, the next morning the wife saw the woman again the same spot, sobbing, and she asked her what the matter was. The woman said that in the field where the farmer was now plowing, she had two children buried, and she was afraid their graves would be dug up. Then she told the wife she had hidden some money in the basement of the farmhouse, and if the wife would go find it, it would be enough for her to have the graves fixed up nicely, with plenty left over.

And, it is said, the couple went out and found the two graves. They also found the money, because they put an iron fence around the burial sites and marked them with special stones. Exactly how much money was found was never determined, but people in the community noticed that the farmer and his wife, who had been considered poor folks by their neighbors, thereafter became known as people of considerable means at the time.

* * * * *

WHERE THE WRAITHS WALKED

No one knows for sure why the wraiths walked at night at old Mt. San Angelo, now part of Sweet Briar College in Amherst County. There are a number of possible reasons, but to this day no one has pinned down an exact explanation. What is known is that for decades this Georgian manor, transformed in 1909 from an Italian Victorian, has been said to be haunted, most prominently by the shadowy figure of "Miss Indy" — Indiana Fletcher Williams, the founder of the college. She is said to have stalked about the rooms in the house where there are white marble fireplaces — the dining room and the upstairs bedroom. Old time residents of the Coolwell area told, too, of seeing, on certain nights, the spectral vision of a decapitated farmhand riding his "terrified mount" down the long winding driveway.

While no rational reason was ever given for either phenomenon, the belief of their existence was so strong that house owners could not get any domestic help to work in the house. In desperation, one family "imported" a maid and her son from Maryland once. But the maid quit in haste one morning because she saw "a white figure bent over my boy while he was sleeping last night."

There are at least three possible causes for such legends. One is that the spirits were unhappy with the renovation of the house which originally dates to 1858. A second was offered by Miss Winifred Walker, whose family lived at Mt. San Angelo from 1909 to 1926. She said her father often told ghost stories to the girls at Sweet Briar, and the retelling of those tales could have added to the lore. And then there were the tragic deaths in the house in the 1930s, when the Revis family lived there. Mrs. Revis, according to local remembrances, had become addicted to drugs after treatment for a serious illness. Her husband hanged himself either in the attic, as some sources say, or from the chandelier in the conservatory, as others told. The Revis butler also was found mysteriously drowned in the lake on the property. Such sad occurrences, coupled with the fact that the large old white house sits on top of a hill, tend to stir superstitious imaginations, and normally could explain the spookiness.

But, contend old timers in the area, the recounting of hauntings at Mt. San Angelo long pre-date the untimely deaths there. And so, the stories persists.

* * * * *

A BEACON FOR LOST LOVE

pring Hill in Amherst County, also known as the Tait House has been in disrepair for decades now — a crumbling shadow of its long ago splendor. And for the past 40, 50, or 60 years, children have played around there, but few have dared go inside, for the old house is supposed to be haunted. The author's cousin, Layton Taylor, used to play there as a boy eons ago, and still remembers it well today.

"It was very scary, even then," he recalls. "There used to be an old trap door leading from the basement to a tunnel. It ran about 30 feet to an ice house and was partially collapsed. I can remember I was down in that tunnel one night with some friends, and as we were coming up the ladder to the trap door we heard heavy booted footsteps on the top of the door. It frightened the hell out of us. We must have waited down there, breathless, in the dark for an hour or more before we dared even move. We never did find out what it was."

The William W. Harpers bought Spring Hill in the 1940s and lived in a small cottage there for time after World War II. They had plans to restore the mansion house, but never got around to it. And there would have been a lot of work to be done. Mrs. Harper said that people thought one of the previous tenants had buried money there somewhere since he had a well known distrust for banks. Consequently, all the mantles and hearths had been pried or dug around, but no money was ever found.

Then there was the inexplicable light which the Harper children saw at night. Mrs. Harper said it was not so much a distinct light, but a "lightness which we could see going into the upstairs hall. We had been told about the ghost," and there were occasions where she admitted that family members would hear footsteps starting up the stairs. The legend was that one of the Tait daughters of a bygone era was in love with a young man, but her father refused to let her marry him. Allegedly, it was she who was heard on the stairs and it was her light — a beacon for her lover — that curiously glowed from an upstairs window in the old house.

Mrs. Harper said the light could have been a reflection since the house had rippled old glass panes, or it could have come from headlights on the highway or from a passing train. But she added that she could never actually determine the source. "We never knew for sure."

* * * * *

THE REAPPEARING BLOODSTAIN

here was, a few years ago, a group of self-described "little old ladies," who pursued a rather intriguing hobby. They activated their common interests in Virginia history and parapsychology by visiting alleged haunted houses in the greater Lynchburg area. To prepare themselves for the possibility of meeting up with a "discarnate spirit," they did deep breathing exercises for relaxation and "sensitization." "We walk from room to room, and when the hair on your arm stands up, you know there's something there," one of them said once in a newspaper interview. One place where this happened was an old house called Ivanhoe in Rustburg, southeast of Lynchburg and southwest of Appomattox. Named after Sir Walter Scott's famous novel, Ivanhoe was built around 1780, at one time served as a tavern and later was converted into a family residence. The ladies toured it because it has long had the reputation of being the most haunted house in Campbell County.

So many forms of psychic phenomena have occurred there, it is difficult to know where to begin. There is, for example, the ever-reappearing bloodstain. Many old houses have had bloodstains which have been troublesome to remove, but the one at Ivanhoe went beyond that. Its origins date to the time, long ago, that a "pedlar" was murdered in one of the upper rooms. From then on, guests were subjected to a wide variety of disturbing manifestations. There were alarming noises, generally late at night. Bedclothes would be yanked off the bed by unseen hands and piled in the middle of the floor. Once, two young men sharing the room swore they saw a pillow fly by them from wall to wall. Guests and family members alike frequently heard the sharp sound of a heavy weight, or body, falling. It was believed to be the pedlar's, but no cause was ever discovered. Oddly, this always happened between nine and ten in the evening, possibly the hour of the foul deed.

Outside, the "heavy strokes of an ax chopping a tree" echoed throughout the house, accompanied by "labored breathing incidental to the exertion of chopping. Again, the phantom woodsman was never sighted. The continuing series of unearthly events caused household problems at Ivanhoe. No servant could be induced to approach or leave the house after dark. Nor could they rid the bloodstain from the floor. Scrubbing it out was useless. Staining would cover it for a short period, then it would magically reappear. Finally, an attempt was made to burn it out, but even that failed.

There was, too, apparently a second spirit in the Rustburg manor — that of a "Lavender Lady." She was seen frequently by residents, often going up or coming down the stairway, and the descriptions were always much the same: a slender, dark-haired woman dressed in lavender, with "a bunch of violets" worn on her breast. Those who passed her said the scent of the flowers was "strong and delightful!" Mrs. Cora Mosby, who lived at Ivanhoe early in this century, once commented, "So unmistakable has been the perfume that I have said to myself, 'what nonsense, there can be no violets at this season'."

One summer afternoon, when the family was away, a man stopped at the house seeking directions. Seeing a woman dressed in lavender on the porch, he approached her only to have the figure vanish before his eyes. Another one-time resident, Anne Rode, told of the time she had gone downstairs to get a book one night and upon going back upstairs she passed another person she assumed to be her sister. She reached out to her, and her hand went *through* the "lifelike" apparition.

No explanation has been offered as to who the delicate lady

might be, or whether she is connected in any way with the unfortunate pedlar. The ladies who in more recent times visited Ivanhoe as a band of amateur psychic investigators could shed no new light on the mystery either. Nor could they say with any specificity why, while walking through the aged rooms in the house, the hair on their arms stood straight up!

* * * * *

A PAIR OF ODD OCCURRENCES

here are at least two time-honored ghost stories in the Lynchburg area which later proved not to be ghostly related at all. Nevertheless, they are colorful in their own right and deserve a brief recounting. They were recalled by Mrs. Margaret Anthony Cabell in her 1858 "Sketches and Recollections of Lynchburg."

One involved a nameless professional gentleman who allegedly was sitting alone in his parlor late one Sunday night when "the front door opened noiselessly, and, there he was aware a tall, pale stranger stood before him, bareheaded and clothed in white garments." Astonished at the apparitional sight, the gentleman recovered enough of his composure to ask the nocturnal visitor what he wanted. In return, the spirit-like character answered in a strange manner. "My name is known only to the Almighty, who has it written in the book of life," he said. "I have no abiding city. I came from the uttermost part of the earth today, and the chariot waits which will tonight covney me I know not whither."

The visitor continued on in a somewhat "wild and incoherent" manner, then abruptly arose, said "peace be to this house and all within it," and then vanished "as noiselessly as he had entered." Within days, the story swept across Lynchburg, gaining embellishment and momentum as it was passed along, to the point where a number of town inhabitants called upon the professional gentleman at this house and demanded to hear, first-hand, the details of the encounter.

Alas, there was a reasonable explanation for the eerie visit. It seems that a man, clad in white, was being escorted from Lynchburg to the lunatic hospital in Williamsburg when he somehow eluded his attendants, escaped for a short while, and wandered off the streets into the host's house. Even after this fact was offered, however, it took a long time for residents to believe that the professional gentleman's visitor was not from another world.

The other occurrence involved "a large white house" on the left of the old Methodist graveyard. It was believed to be on the west side of Washington Street. The location of this particular dwelling was said to be "melancholy," and, consequently, it was hard to get it tenanted. It was for a time inhabited by several poor families, and there were persistent reports that "strange and awful noises" eminated from a small upstairs room.

According to the occupant of that room, he was once visited by a "strange man, in a voluminous, old-fashioned, white great coat." He supposedly told the startled lodger that he had been murdered, and if one would look in the small room in the back of the house, he would find the blood stains to prove his case. As the story leaked out, it caused a small sensation with "crowds going to the house to see the blood-stained floor, and to listen to the horrid recital." In fact, some actually paid to see the room.

Encouraged by the attention, the lodger continued to build upon his spectral tale until the enormity of the crime reached almost unbelieveable heights. But eventually, a hoax was unveiled when it was learned that the "murder chamber" had previously been the packing room of a large pork dealer, and the lodger himself, on former occasions, had "not been at all scrupulous about telling the truth, particularly when anything could be made by the contrary."

* * * * *

A TIMELY SPECTRAL SIGHTING

ost Lynchburg area ghosts are old ghosts. Most of them have been known at least since the 19th century, and others even before that. The story of "Miss Cornelia," however, only surfaced a few years ago, in fact in the mid-1970s. The house location and the family who experienced her ethereal return are not known, because the people involved requested anonymity, which is not an uncommon occurrence. But this story does include a couple of unusual twists. One concerns a rare apparitional sighting, and the other involves the date on which this phenomena was observed.

The house is known to be at least a century and a half old, because Miss Cornelia Clopton was born in it sometime around 1850, the daughter of a Baptist minister. The present day family moved in sometime in 1968 and almost immediately began experiencing

Cornelia's gentle spirit. There were odd noises for which no source could be found. There was, too, the man of the house said, "some undefinable presence." He said the family joked about it. "We'd say, it's a ghost, because, you know, an old house should have one."

One the night of April 4, 1974, it rained very hard. The next morning the man was awakened early, and recalled later, "You know how sometimes you just know someone is in the house." It was precisely 5 a.m. He knew this because the clock had just struck. Quietly, so as not to disturb the others, he got up and went to the top of the stairs. All was deathly still.

Then he was quoted as saying, "I noticed that at the bottom of the stairs, it looked awfully light." He reasoned that it could have been a neighbor's garage light left on overnight, but he could see the garage next door through a window and realized the light wasn't coming from there. As he stared, transfixed, the mysterious light began to concentrate and take a shape. Slowly, it developed into the distinct shape of an old woman. "I was absolutely horrified," he said. "My arms went numb and I was freezing. It didn't give off light, but it had a light of its own. It was a woman, about five feet tall with her hair up and a long skirt and full leg o'mutton sleeves." He said the woman never looked up and never spoke, then moved to another room, out of sight. When he cautiously descended the stairs, the wraith-like form was no where to be seen. No doors were opened and shut and no windows were open, but there was nothing.

At this point, the family, which had known Miss Cornelia had lived in the house more than a half century before, decided to do some research. They learned that the woman, then in her 60s, had made a trip to Minnesota in the spring of 1917 to visit her aged parents. Just before she was scheduled to come home, she became ill with the flu and died on March 26. She had left specific instructions that her body was to be returned to Lynchburg, and she was buried in the Spring Hill cemetery on April 8th. Through more checking, the family learned that Miss Cornelia's body probably arrived back in town on April 5th. After more digging, it was discovered that in 1917 an early train arrived in Lynchburg at 5 a.m. on the 5th.

Thus the singular sighting of Miss Cornelia's apparition had been made 57 years later — at precisely the same time and on the same date that she had returned home!

A Sad Case of Precognition

Precognition, loosely, means the ability of a person to get accurate information from the future, most generally in the form of a vision or dream. While this form of psychic phenomena occurs more often than many others, it nevertheless still is one of the least understood aspects of the overall field of parapsychology. Grimly, many "flashes" of precognition contain warnings of impending disaster, injury, or death.

One of the most famous such instances involved the foreboding dream of death envisioned by Abraham Lincoln shortly before his assassination. In his case, it was a recurring dream which so disturbed him that he looked for answers in his Bible. "I turned to other passages, and seemed to encounter a dream or a vision wherever I looked, " he said. "I kept on turning the leaves of the old book, and everywhere my eye fell upon passages recording matters strangely in keeping with my own thoughts — supernatural visitations, dreams, visions, etc."

At one point, Lincoln detailed his dream to his wife, Mary Todd Lincoln. He did it in a deliberate slow and sad countenance. "About ten days ago," he said, "I retired late. I soon began to dream. There seemed to be a death-like stillness about me. Then I heard subdued sobs, as if a number of people were weeping. I thought I left my bed and wandered downstairs. There the silence was broken by the same pitiful sobbing, but the mourners were invisible. I went from room to room; no living person was in sight, but the same mournful sounds of distress met me as I passed along."

Lincoln continued: "It was light in all the rooms; every object was familiar to me; but where were all the people who were grieving as if their hearts would break? I was puzzled and alarmed. What could be the meaning of all this? Determined to find the cause of a state of things so mysterious and so shocking, I kept on until I arrived at the East Room (of the White House), which I entered.

Before me was a catafalque, on which rested a corpse wrapped in funeral vestments. Around it were stationed soldiers who were acting as guards; and there was a throng of people, some gazing mournfully upon the corpse, whose face was covered, others weeping pitifully.

"'Who is dead in the White House?' I demanded of one of the soldiers. 'The President,' was his answer. 'He was killed by an assassin.' Then came a loud burst of grief from the crowd, which awoke me from my dream. I slept no more that night; and although it was only a dream, I have been strangely annoyed by it ever since."

Following Lincoln's death, Mrs. Lincoln was distraught with horror, and it is said her first coherent exclamation was, "His dream was prophetic."

In and around Lynchburg, there are two similar incidences of precognition heralding an imminently forthcoming death. One was recorded in 1858 by Mrs. Margaret Anthony Cabell in "Sketches and Recollections of Lynchburg by the Oldest Inhabitant." She told of a distinguished lawyer named Daniel Sheffey from Staunton. For years, he travelled twice a year to Lynchburg to attend the Chancery courts presided over by Judge Creed Taylor (sic). After one such session, held every May and October, Sheffey dined with friends and then retired to the Franklin Hotel to spend the night.

At some point during the early morning hours, Sheffey awoke, and was visibly shaken. He awakened a colleague named Peachy Gilmer and told him that he had just had a most distressing dream. Gilmer said to take no stock in dreams and to go back to sleep. But an hour later, Sheffey arose again, shook Gilmer to consciousness, and told him he had the same dream again. This time he related the dream. "I dreamed that I was on my way to Staunton," he said, "and that I stopped for a time at my farm in Augusta, some miles from my home. I was sitting by the door of the farmhouse when I saw a very singular appearance in the clouds, which floated on the air, till the apparition was so near as for me distinctly to see and recognize the features of my beloved wife, who, with a mournful countenance and deep, solemn voice, waved to me her hand, saying 'Farewell, we have parted never again to meet on earth."

Sheffey left the next morning to return to Staunton. Within 72 hours, word was received in Lynchburg that he had died very suddenly at his farm near Staunton . . . "never again," in the words of Mrs. Cabell, "beholding his happy home and devoted family."

* * * * *

The second occurrence of a precursor of death involved a young boy of 15, Edmund Henry, son of Judge Samuel Hugh Henry of Amherst Courthouse. This story is much more familiar to long-time residents of the area and has been told and retold through the years, including a thorough account in Margaret DuPont Lee's book "Virginia Ghosts," published in 1930. It was often related by Mildred Henry, Edmund's sister.

Of Judge Henry's four sons, it seems Edmund was the brightest and best looking, but he also was so full of mischief that he often got into scraps with the village boys, and his school grades were so bad they drove his father, a widower, to distraction. Edmund was constantly being lectured and disciplined.

One evening the Judge was entertaining some friends in the house and he banished Edmund to the parlor to study his lessons. Some time later, the housemaid came to Miss Henry in an agitated state and told her that she had heard "peculiar noises" in the parlor, and that when she opened the door to discern the cause, she found Edmund standing up and looking "very frightened." When she spoke to him he would not answer. Mildred Henry then went to the parlor to check and later said Edmund "appeared terrified, was deathly pale, and seemed not to be able to speak." Alarmed, she ran to the library and told her father. "I spoke to him and he did not notice me," she said. "His hands and face were as cold as ice." Then she cried.

Judge Henry was not amused. He thought Edmund was just up to one of his tricks, but to alleviate his daughter's obvious concern, he excused himself from his guests and went to the parlor. He found Edmund "looking deathly white" and staring intently at one corner of the room. He seemed not to have noticed his father's presence, and, in Miss Henry's words, it was as if he was "frozen to stone."

The judge spoke to him, but Edmund did not reply. He continued to stare at the far corner of the room, as if entranced. There appeared to be a strange spell over him. Then the judge told other members of the family to leave the room, and he sat down on the sofa with Edmund, put his arm around him, and soothingly asked him what was the matter.

After an indeterminable amount of time, Edmund finally spoke. "Father," he sobbed, "I have seen mother. I am afraid you will not believe me, but she came to me and spoke to me." The judge asked him if he was sure he had not fallen asleep and was dreaming, and Edmund assured him he had been wide awake. He said he had been doing his lessonwork when "I felt there was someone in the room. I could neither write nor move. I looked around and saw no one, but in the corner behind the piano I saw something like a white hand-kerchief lying on the floor, and as I looked at it, it seemed to move and to grow larger. I watched it as it grew larger and larger, until it was the size of a grown person. Then it moved from behind the piano and advanced toward me.

"I tried to run," Edmund continued, "but could not move. As it came near, I saw that it was a woman. Her hair was black and her eyes were lookng right at me and I recognized my mother. she came up to me and leaning over me, put her arms around me and said, 'Try to be a good boy, my son, and meet me in heaven; it won't be long.' Then she disappeared.

In the days thereafter, Edmund was a changed boy. He stopped fighting, made friends with the village boys, improved his school grades to straight A's, and joined the church. He told his father that his mother had wanted him to join her in heaven and he intended to keep his promise to her to do that.

Not long after that, on a hot day in August, Edmund went to the river to go swimming with his brothers and some friends. His sister asked him to run an errand for her in the village, and when he returned to the river, he was overheated. He dived into the water, was immediately seized by cramps, and drowned before anyone could reach him.

The Extraordinary Rocking Cradle

(Author's note: From the beginnings of my research for this book, everytime I had talked about the Lynchburg area, people would mention the "Rocking Cradle House." They would say that I had to include a story on this, because it was the most famous haunted house in the city. Everyone, it seemed had heard about the house, but seemingly no one could provide any details on where it was, or when the phenomena occurred.

Finally, in a book called "The Oldest Living Resident of Lynchburg - 1858," by Mrs. Margaret Cabell, there was a specific reference to the rocking cradle, but even here the facts were obscure. The incident was said to have happened in 1839, but Mrs. Cabell was so sure that everyone had heard about it by then that she failed to discuss the particulars.

Eventually, the trail led to the Lynchburg Public Library, where there were a couple of 40-year-old newspaper clippings that mentioned the cradle that rocked by itself. Then, there was a chapter in Margaret DuPont Lee's 1930 book, "Virginia ghosts," entitled "Telekenesis in Lynchburg." It covered a plethora of psychic manifestations which took place at a house "at the corner of Jackson and Eleventh Streets in Lynchburg." Could this be the house? One of the newspaper articles, published in 1951, said the house was located at 1104 Jackson Street.

Next, I went upstairs over the Lynchburg Library to the Jones Memorial Library, one of the best sources of geneological material in Virginia. After checking on a number of stories in Amherst County, I casually mentioned to the librarian if he had heard of the rocking cradle house and did he have any information on it. He smiled and said as a matter of fact, he did. And then he brought me a copy of

Works Progress Administration (WPA) of Virginia Historical Inventory Research Report. It was part of depression-era project sponsored by the Virginia Conservation Commission under the direction of its Division of History.

The report was titled, simply, "The Poston Home." It had been written June 3, 1937, by Susan R. Beardsworth. As I turned the pages of the report, I had to restrain myself from getting up and shouting "Eureka!" There it was! On page two, under the heading, "Historical Significance," were the magic words I had been searching for: "This house," wrote Susan Beardsworth, "is of interest chiefly because of the legends and ghost stories connected with it, the best known of which is the spring of 1839. The house is generally known as 'the house where the cradle rocked'."

Such a "find," is to a writer the rough equivalent to a treasure hunter uncovering a cache of gold coins.

The Poston House is named for W. C. Poston who bought the property in 1902. It is not known exactly when the house was built. Says Ms. Beardsworth: "The property passed through so many hands in the early days that it is impossible to determine who built it, but a careful study of all records on this and surrounding property and a comparison of dates and amounts involved in the sales, would strongly indicate it having been built about 1819, by Edmund B.

Norvell, or by Thomas Wyatt, before 1813.

"This story and a half brick house originally faced on the Salem Turnpike, which is now 12th Street, and was built in three sections The main one consisting of two rooms with a closed center stairway on the first floor, and two rooms and hall on the second floor. On either corner of the back yard were the other two sections, one a two room office, the other a two room kitchen, all built of brick. The house has been remodelled or rebuilt twice; in 1875, the office was torn down and incorporated in the main structure, and in 1904, the kitchen was also built into the house, forming a wing, so now there are eight rooms and two halls.

"It is all very plain, simple and quaint looking, the only one of its kind left standing in the city."

Ms. Lee, in her book, says the house at the corner of Jackson and Eleventh Steets was built about 1840 by a Colonel James Maurice Langhorne, which is in dispute with Ms. Beardsworth's account. Yet a cradle that rocked on its own is also mentioned as one of the supernatural events that took place at the house. Is it the same house, or were there two different houses involved?

The residence Ms. Lee discusses was "dreadfully haunted," according to William Nelson Wellford, Colonel Langhorne's grandson. "The ghosts were at work as far back as I can remember," he wrote Mrs. Lee. Wellford's sister, Mrs. John Wallace, added: "The remarkable phenomena were so numerous and of such frequency she could by no means recollect them all." She did remember her mother telling her that she had seen servants in the house drop on their knees and exclaim: "Oh God! A ghost brushed by me."

Mrs. Wallace's mother also said that on "numerous occasions" after the servants had finished their chores in the kitchen, late in the afternoon, and everything was cleaned up and secured, she would hear all sorts of noises coming from the area. She said it sounded like a group of servants preparing for a great banquet. There were hurried footsteps back and forth across the floor; the opening and shutting of doors, and the rattling of china and silver among other things. Subsequent investigations would reveal posts and pans strewn all about, pantry and kitchen range doors open, flour and sugar spilled, and in general, "everything in confusion." Never, did Mrs. Wallace's mother, or anyone else in the house, ever find a rational explanation for such activities.

At other times, the Wallaces found beds unsheeted," linen and bedclothes piled in a bundle in the center of the floor, and the rooms in a "state of utter confusion." Mrs. Wallace's mother also had seen keys in an old leather basket kept on the side of the table, jump up and down "as if someone was shaking the basket violently." Mrs. Wallace herself saw "the walls shake up and down, and felt it, too." When two young nephews came to witness the strange goings on, they became so frightened by the manifestations, including "unseen hands touching them," that they abruptly left. Welford added that the phenomena became so frequent and so frightening, that no one would buy or rent the house for a long time.

The major account of the rocking cradle house, however, came from testimony given by Trueheart Poston to Ms. Beardsworth. He was the son of the man who bought the house in 1902, and he was an architect. Here is what Poston had to say: "The following are some legends and stories connected with the house at 1104 Jackson Street . . . Mr. Asbury Christian in his book, 'Lynchburg and Its People,' gives the account of the rocking cradle. . . . The house at that time (1839) was occupied by a Rev. Smith, who was a cousin of Bishop Early. I do not know whether this cradle belonged to the Smith's or was loaned them by the Early's, but the tale has it that the Rev. Smith, upon returning home from his duties, found the Negro mammy in a state of hysteria and was told that the cradle had been rocking with the baby in it for some hours and would not stop.

"Upon hearing this, Rev. Smith went into the room and found that the cradle was indeed rocking. Being a very religious man, he commanded the cradle to stop rocking in the name of Beelzebub, whereupon the cradle immediately stopped. Rev. Smith then suggested that Beelzebub start rocking the cradle again, whereupon he apparently did so. This constant rocking under orders continued for a period of some days, during which, as the rumors spread, most of the town folk dropped by and witnessed this sight for themselves. (One "contemporary account" of the event states that "hundreds closed their places of business" and went to see the rocking cradle.) Apparently, after just so long, the cradle ceased rocking and would rock only by human efforts from then on.

"The cradle itself is a very beautiful Sheraton mahogany high poster affair with turned spindle sides and a field bed canopy. It gives the effect of being a minature Sheraton field bed on rockers.

"There is another tale," Poston continued, "which apparently had its origin with Mr. Walter Addison, who was, up to the time of his death, about 10 years ago, editor of the Lynchburg News. The house was in our possession at the time, and Mr. and Mrs. Addison were staying with us. They occupied a downstairs bedroom at the foot of the steps. Mr. Addison would generally return home at two

or three o'clock in the morning after checking over his editorial for the morning paper. Upon one of these occasions, he opened the door and saw, on the landing, an old lady, apparently about 80 years old, dressed in a rather old fashioned costume and it being very late and he imagining she was probably deaf, merely nodded and went into his room, naturally assuming that she was some relative of ours.

"The next morning at breakfast when no such lady appeared, Mr. Addison asked my mother if aunt was not well. Of course, there was no such person visiting us at the time and the rumor has gotten around that the old lady is a constant and cheerful ghost occupant of the house. I cannot recall any person having seen her since that date, although many visitors report that they are sure they have heard her moving her feet and heard the cushions in chairs sink as though she were sitting and noticed such other sounds as might be made by such a lady.

"There is also the story connected with a major in the Confederate Army who at one time lived here. . . . What with material losses caused by the war and the general tendency which some men have towards alcohol, the major eventually got to the delirium tremens stage in his drinking and upon such occasions was locked in the dining room by his family.

"During his periods of intoxication, it was his habit to beat his way out with a poker or any handy object. The woodwork in this room shows the results of his attempts at freedom in a very obvious manner. All woodwork around various windows and doors show evidence of where the major had inserted his poker to pry loose the locks and also evidence of where apparently at the height of his rages, he took great pleasure in merely pounding the woodwork with his poker.

"Various rumors have arisen in connection with this episode, chiefly concerning the fact that at midnight the doors from this room would all open whether locked or not. When we bought the place in 1902, the original batten doors were still in place, though sadly chewed by the major's poker. Not believing the tale of the opening doors, my parents spent their first night in the first floor bedroom, only to be awakened promptly at 12 o'clock by the creaking of two doors, which they had securely latched before retiring. It appears that at slightly irregular intervals, these same two doors would invariably unlatch themselves and open in a very slow and creaking fashion, as though the major had finally won his freedom.

"I cannot recall any other tales concerning the house," Poston concluded, "except a very vague rumor of a body which drops out of an upstairs dormer. I have not been able to find out whether there is a qualified event for this tale, but do know that for a long time during my boyhood, I was constantly terrified by a sound such as a body dropping out of the windows."

CHAPTER 22

The Carnival of Death

ave we, as humans, always been fascinated with the morbid side of life? Perhaps. Today, violence and death can be witnessed any night of the week on television, network as well as cable. Some of the biggest blockbuster movies — the Rambos and Terminators — seem to be the ones which can create the greatest amount of blood letting and destruction. But this should come as no surprise. Did not the Romans relish such horrific spectacles as lions tearing apart the flesh of men, and of gladiators, like game cocks, battling till one kills the other?

And so it was, in history, with public executions. Can one imagine, today, taking the family out to the courthouse square to witness a public beheading, or a hanging as a form of entertainment? Such was the case in Lynchburg around 1830, when a man named J. M. Jones attracted the attention of thousands. This curious historical vignette was described by W. Asbury Christian in his Book, "Lynchburg and Its People," published in 1900.

Jones had killed a man named George Hamilton on a boat in the Lynchburg area in 1828 and the newspapers had a field day, stirring up a great deal of excitement. In fact, the publicity was so widespread for that era that 200 persons were challenged before a jury could be seated. High-powered lawyers of the day represented both the defense and the prosecution, and Jones eventually was found guilty and sentenced to hang.

The condemned man received one reprieve, but as Christian put it in his book, "he was to pay the extreme penalty of the law." The public interest which had built during the trial phase, exploded. "The day of doom had scarcely dawned when the people began to pour into the town, some in buggies, some in wagons, some in ox-carts, others on horseback, and hundreds a-foot," Christian wrote.

"It looked like a circus day; the women had on their best gowns and their meeting-going bonnets, the men were dressed in their

Sunday clothes, best hats and new shoes. Business was almost at a standstill, for it seemed that the town and the country had turned out to the carnival of death." The crowd was estimated at 15,000! Christian reported that "boys were laughing and whistling, women were smiling, and men were laughing and chatting; all seemed to be in a good mood except one."

Precisely at Noon, the jail opened, and "out walked a pale, sad looking man between two guards. They mounted the wagon standing at the jail door and the prisoner sat upon the plain pine coffin that was in it. Then came the Artillery, the Rifles, the reverend clergy and a large number of citizens. The line of march was up Clay to Fifth, thence to the Methodist graveyard, and down the hill near Tate's old mill. The hillsides were black with people eager to witness the execution. When the gallows was reached, the ghastly exercises *were opened with singing!*"

Next, a prayer was led by a Presbyterian Reverend, followed by an "appropriate sermon" preached by an Episcopal minister, and lastly a "feeling address" was made by a Methodist clergyman. This long procession and program went on for more than three hours.

Jones himself, possibly delaying for time in hopes of a last minute miracle, spoke briefly.

And then the moment came. The noose was placed around his neck, the cap was fixed, and the trap door was sprung. "Horror of horrors!" Christian wrote, "the rope broke, and he had to be hanged again." Grotesquely, he remained hanging for nearly an hour in full view of the great crowd. At length, he was taken down and carried into the old mill. Some say an autopsy was performed. Said Christian in 1900: "What an awful effect a public execution of this kind must have had upon the people. Surely, the present generation is wiser than their fathers, in having all executions private." But from the descriptions given, it sounded more like a day of interest and macabre enjoyment than an awful effect. That is, for everyone except the poor Mr. Jones.

Christian added a spectral footnote to this chilling episode. "The Negroes who lived near there (the old mill) said that every night after that (when Jones body was taken there) a light appeared in the mill, and the windows rattled, until something in white came to the window and threw a *man's skin* into the pond. The haunted mill was an object of terror to them after dark!"

CHAPTER 23

Some Ghosts that Should Have Been

* * * * *

QUIXOTIC QUICK HOUSE

o some oldtimers in Amherst County, it is still known as the Edward Hill House. Hill had the two story red brick structure built about 200 years ago and successive generations of the family lived in it. With a formal portico and with vines and scrubs covering part of the exterior, it has all the outward apearances of a proper colonial residence befitting a gentleman of Hill's stature. Inside, a central hall leads to rooms finished in cherrywood with handsome carvings around the mantels and at the stair ends. Over the years the original basement kitchen became a furnace room; the basement dining room a playroom; and the old wine cellar a storeroom.

But to most residents in and around Madison Heights, about three and a half miles north of Lynchburg, the place is simply known as Quick House, named after another family that lived there. And for longer than anyone living can now remember, Quick House was known not only to be haunted, but to be literally infested with a variety of spirited manifestations that have triggered back stove gossip in the area for years. Such activities have been the subject of numerous newspaper articles, magazine pieces, and were included in Agnes Rothery's descriptively lovely book, "Houses Virginians Have Loved."

The range of psychic phenomena is curiously varied at Quick House. There are the more or less standard mysterious footsteps made by unseen feet up and down the stairs and in second floor rooms. There are a woman's sobs, often heard outside a particular bedroom door, whether or not any woman is in the house, and for which there is never found any rational source. There is, or was, a sewing machine, which on numerous occasions sworn to by witnesses, would run by itself, as if guided by phantom hands. A generation and a half ago, say children who lived in the house at the time, a riderless white horse would gallop in dizzying circles about the house on certain moonlit nights. There were times when past owners complained about leaving the house locked tight, only to return hours later to find rooms all in disarray with furniture moved about randomly. A cradle rocks by itself. There is one room in which a window refuses to stay up. And, finally, there is another room in which the lighting "goes crazy." Whenever a candle was lit in this room it immediately went out, although there was no breeze or draft of air to extinguish it. And occupants of the house have had continuous trouble with electric lights in this room ever since they were first installed in the early part of the century. In an Amherst New Era Progress article published nearly 20 years ago, Dot Machares, who grew up in Quick House, told a reporter that no matter how many times the wiring had been redone in the room, the family still had trouble with the lights.

The house today is owned by the E. W. Woodys, and they do not talk about the strange goings on there, but this has only helped fuel the stories which have evolved over the years. The difference between Quick House and many other old haunted homes is that while the accounts of a particular manifestation may vary from time to time, depending on who is relating the tale, the fascinating legend behind all the phenomena remains intact, with little deviation.

It centers around what had been described by many as a "rich and beautiful" bereaved widow who lived in the house long ago. While no name has been associated with this young woman, who was also said to be "wicked," and no time frame has been determined, it is likely she lived in the house sometime during the first half of the 19th century, and more probably sometime between the 1820s and the 1850s.

There is a consensus of opinion that at some point during this general period she travelled to New orleans by way of St. louis, and during her visit there she was so taken with an exceptionally beautiful light-skinned woman at a slave auction that she bought her on the spot to be her personal maid. Back at the Quick House, it didn't take the widow's jeolousy long to rage. She began beating and whipping her new charge for even the slightest offense, perceived or otherwise.

At this time a handsome and quite eligible bachelor named George Landrum entered the scene. He came calling on the widow, but she was fast to notice his admiration for the "dark, unearthly beauty" of the maid, even though he made no overt advances towards her. It got so bad that everytime Landrum left after a social call, the widow's whippings of her servant became more "violent and prolonged."

Once, in fact, the girl ran to Landrum as he approached the house, obviously frightened, muttered something to him in French, then she ran into the house only to be severely lashed by the widow's whip. This so sickened the young man that he immediately mounted his horse and left, and didn't call on the widow again for months. Eventually, however, he relented and accepted an invitation to tea. This time as he rode up, he heard sobbing in the summerhouse and stopped to see who was crying and why.

It was the slave girl. She clasped her arms around his knees, but he loosened them and proceeded into the house for tea. Upset by the girl's cowering fear, he left soonafter. But as he headed down the drive he became overcome by what author Rothery described as a "presentiment of evil so overpowering" that he turned and went back. Outside the house, the slave girl came running out to meet him.

In a frantic, breathless mixture of Creole French and English, the girl told Landrum that as soon as he had left, her mistress came after her with a long table knife. She managed to elude the woman, grabbed a pair of garden shears lying on a table as she ran through the hall, and rushed upstairs to a room. The wind immediately blew out the lone candle there. This is the same room at Quick House in which candles still won't burn and the electric lights go haywire. The widow entered the darkened room with the knife held high in her hand, "uttering horrible snarls of rage." As her eyes grew accustomed to dim light coming in from the door, shw saw the slave girl and lunged at her. Terrified, the girl struck back with the shears. They found their mark, the widow screamed and fell to the floor. That was when the girl ran out of the house and into the arms of Landrum.

Realizing the hopelessness of the girl's predicament, the gentleman hoisted her onto the horse and started to gallop off. But the widow's scream had been heard. She was found quickly, and Landrum and the slave girl soon were overtaken. The girl was dragged, screaming, back into the house and locked in one of the downstairs front rooms. In desperation, she tore at the window sash until it gave way, raised the window, slid to the ground and ran down a path leading to the river. Crazed with fear, she leaped from a boulder into the fast flowing river, even though she could not swim. Her body was found two days later floating in the eddy below the dam.

There is an ironic twist to this tragic tale. Later, Landrum learned from a woman who had come to Lynchburg from New Orleans, that the drowned girl was, in fact, not a slave at all. An old Creole who had recently died confessed this on his death bed. The girl actually had been the unwanted daughter of "indiscreet and youthful parents" who had tried to conceal her birth by giving her to a trusted slave to bring up. When that slave had died, the girl somehow fell into the hands of a trader who had sold her to the widow on the auction block. Meanwhile, the real parents, both from "the first families" of Louisiana, had sought in vain to find their child and had only recently traced her to Quick House in Lynchburg.

The widow recovered from her wounds, but from that time on, mysterious happenings began to occur in the house. Much of the phenomena fits the description of a spectral return of the beautiful slave girl. It could explain the soft sobs heard, the footsteps on the stairs, and the fact that no candle could remain lit in the upstairs room where the widow and the girl slashed out at each other.

It could explain, too, another eerie occurrence. It is said that when the western sun strikes the windows in the front of the house they turn to gold. It is a phenomenon so extraordinary that passing motorists have pulled over to the side of the road to stare and wonder.

Such is the legacy of the Creole slave who really wasn't a slave and who lived such an unhappy existence at haunted Quick House.

* * * * *

The only problem with the ghost in the Quick House is that it is not real. It was made up. A hoax! The story had been published and republished in area newspapers for years, and was included in detail in at least two books by respected authors. It seemed like virtually every Halloween, when roundups of area spiritual happenings were printed, the Quick House was always included.

Yet, said Mrs. J. L. Tyler, in a 1970 article in the Lynchburg News, the whole story was fabricated. Mrs. Quick, Mrs. Tyler said, told her about it one night during a visit to the house. She said that she and her husband entertained a doctor and his wife one evening and, as a game, they concocted a story to which each person contributed to. The doctor was so enamored with the outcome that he wrote it up and had it published in a Sunday School paper. And that, apparently, is how others picked it up. "Personally, I think it is time someone buried that pitiful little ghost with the truth," Mrs. Tyler said.

* * * * *

'A MELANCHOLY EPISODE'

hy were there no ghosts looming around the old Lynchburg city cemetery in 1897, when several of the graves were robbed and corpses were spirited away in barrels? It was in that year that "rumors of sinister activities in the cemetery in the dead of night began to spread, causing terror among white and colored people whose relatives were buried there," according to the book "Behind the Brick Wall . . . A Cemetery Story," published in 1968 by the Lynchburg Committee of the National Society of Colonial Dames of America. In a chapter headed "A Melancholy Episode," the report noted that "newly buried bodies were disinterred by stealth, carried to the tool house, and prepared for shipment in barrels to some medical center."

Once word got around about the gruesome goings on, fear spread quickly, and "frightened crowds gathered by night in the cemetery to keep watch over their dead." Many people, in fact, demanded that family graves be opened to prove their loved ones had not been taken or tampered with. As the book quoted, "anxious relatives watched as each spade full of earth was thrown aside. Such a scene had never been witnessed in the old graveyard. This scene was repeated night after night as the belief spread that grave robbery was rife."

Matters reached the boiling point in late February when a destitute young woman names Ella Jamieson committed suicide and was buried in the Potter's field at the expense of the city. At the funeral service, the only mourner present was the girl's father who had *walked* all the way from Appomattox to, as he put it, "see the last of his wayward daughter."

A day later, police stopped a Negro driver and questioned him about a barrel he was to deliver to the railway station. He confessed that in the barrel were the freshly dug up remains of the unfortunate Ms. Jamieson. Under a barrage of questioning, the driver added that he and others had unearthed 11 other bodies. Cemetery superintendent N. J. Farmer was arrested, but later acquitted when he said he had been acting under instructions of the state anatomical board. The body snatching came to an end and Ella Jamieson was reburied.

*****

THE PHANTOM OF THE ROTUNDA

hy are there no ghosts associated with the Rotunda, or with any other buildings on the campus of the University of Virginia? One might imagine the Man himself, Thomas Jefferson, coming back to view his architectural handiwork at the school, some of which was unfinished when he died July 4, 1826. He had such an interest in the construction right up to the end. But there are no stories of spectral Jeffersonian visits. He must have been satisfied with how things turned out.

What about Edgar Allen Poe? There are tales of his apparitional appearance at Talavera in Richmond, and there are even sketchy accounts that he has resurfaced at Ft. Monroe, but all is quiet at UVA. Curious.

There was a report, years ago, that a "Phantom of the Rotunda" haunted the great domed building. According to one newspaper account, this ethereal being desappeared with all the books when the university's library was moved to the new Alderman building in 1938. It must have been a literary ghost.

The only semblance of an inexplicable presence at the home of the Cavaliers is an occasional mention of a former faculty member who certainly would have a stong case for coming back to haunt. His name was John A. G. Davis. When a riot broke out on campus in 1836, Davis, chairman of the faculty, helped quell the violence, winning the respect of both professors and students alike.

Four years later, two young students armed with pistols, roamed about the university grounds one November evening firing blanks and shouting in their own, ill-conceived mini celebration of the riot of '36. Both students wore elaborate disguises and neither was recognizable to fellow classmates. At least one of them wore a Calico mask. One publication said, "they disguised themselves with much secrecy as if they premeditated some dark deed."

Attracted by the ruckus, Professor Davis, who had been on the Lawn, approached the two men, one of whom weighed barely 100 pounds. As Davis neared, this student loaded his pistol with a ball and a charge, and then the chairman scuffled with him in an attempt to rip his mask off, the young man eluded Davis's grasp, backed up a few steps, turned and fired his weapon. The ball struck Davis in the stomach, and as he collapsed, his assailant ran down the Lawn and disappeared into the night.

The wound was at first thought minor, but Davis's condition deteriorated rapidly, and he died two days later. Joseph G. Semmes, a student from Washington, Georgia, subsequently was arrested for the shooting although he never stood trial. Following numerous continuances and delays, Semmes, in poor health, was freed on $25,000 bond. He promptly left town, and was said to have committed suicide in Georgia. This ended what was called "the darkest period in the university's history."

There was at least one account that said the ghost of Davis "may still be wandering in the area of Jefferson and 7th streets." His oldest son, Eugene, lived on that corner in a house owned by his mother-in-law. Late at night it was alleged that the family could hear the latch on the gate open and footsteps on the path to the cottage — but no one was ever seen. Some speculated it could have been either Davis, back to seek justice; or Semmes, returning to clear his conscience.

* * * * *

WHERE IS WOODROW WILSON?

hy is there no ghost of Woodrow Wilson stalking about the old Greek Revival house on North Coalter Street in Staunton, where the 28th President of the United States was born in 1856? True, Wilson's family only lived there for two and a half years before moving on to Augusta, Georgia. Wilson's father was a Presbyterian minister.

It is said that the former President's spirit indeed lingers on in the house where he died just off Embassy Row in Washington, D.C. He moved there in 1921, after completing two terms as Chief Executive and was in failing health. Servants and close associates said that Wilson suffered frequent lapses of memory while at the house and what were described as "unpredictable crying spells."

Soon after he died, the caretaker at the house reported occasionally hearing the "slow shuffle" of a man with a cane climbing the stairs. Others swore they heard the muffled sounds of a man's sobs. One day a cleaning lady entered the bedroom, looked up, and said she saw a "bespectacled figure" sitting in the President's favorite rocking chair. She said the figure looked exactly like President Wilson. She blinked and the vision vanished, but the empty chair continued to rock back and forth.

One might wonder why Wilson's spirit — if that is what it was — chose the house in Washington to return to; a house where he had often been sad in his declining years over failure to carry out some of his life-long objectives. Rather, why didn't he come back to his boyhood home in Staunton where, as a toddler, he only knew carefree happiness?

Does a Ghost Guard the Beale Treasure

he ghost of Thomas Jefferson Beale — if there is one — must either be crying in complete, total, absolute frustration . . . or laughing so hard his sides ache. Beale, you see, is the Virginia gentleman, or hooligan, and there are strong arguments for either choice, who is said to have buried a legendary horde of gold, silver and precious gems somewhere near the town of Bedford, west of Lynchburg. The cache allegedly included nearly 3,000 pounds of gold, more than 5,000 pounds of silver, and hundreds of thousands of dollars worth of jewels. According to the legend, Beale and his associates buried the treasure in iron pots in the ground, leaving behind a complex code, which, once broken would reveal the precise location of their loot.

But nearly 175 years later, a burning question remains unanswered: was any treasure buried at all, or did Beale pull off one of the greatest hoaxes in history? If he did, his spirit must be rolling in laughter at the thousands — thousands — of people who have searched in vain, some squandering their own life savings in the process, for the pots of gold. But if he really did hide a fortune, then he must weep ghostly tears because no one has been able to find even a single coin.

Whether, in fact, Beale buried anything at all has become almost anti-climatic because even if it was proven he didn't, undoubtedly there would be legions of amateur adventurers who would never believe it, and would keep on digging. Because over the years the Beale treasure has almost become bigger than life. It has been the subject of countless newspaper and magazine articles, books and television programs — to the point where it is beginning to rival some of the top unsolved mysteries of all times, such as the Lost

Dutchman mine in Arizona, and the eternal search for the Abominable Snowman. It certainly must qualify as Virginia's most enduring and alluring mystery.

The enigmatic Thomas J. Beale is believed to have been born around 1792. Some who have written about him described him as "a gentleman well educated, evidently of good family, and with popular manners." Others have said he was a black sheep, "gun slinging genius" who was constantly bailed out of scrapes by his more respectable brothers. There is one account that, as a young man, Beale shot and killed a man in Fincastle, Virginia, which led, indirectly to his finding of a king's ransom out west. Beale claimed, however, that he and 30 individuls "of good character" were "seeking adventure" when they left on a two-year expedition hunting buffaloes and grizzlies. The year was 1817.

It still is a puzzle as to exactly where this curious troop of Virginians wound up in the west. Some have said New Mexico, some Arizona, and some "south-central Colorado." There is no concensus, but most researchers feel Beale and the others were somewhere in the vicinity north of Santa Fe when they discovered gold in a small ravine. They mined it for several months and then their pile grew so large they became apprehensive. So the men designated Beale to lead a small contingent back with the gold to bury it in Bedford County, in a remote area between the mountains. Their trust in Beale apparently was without question.

And so, in November 1819, Beale arrived back home with two wagon loads of gold and silver nuggets. In the Goose Creek area, Beale followed a narrow and seldom-used trail leading into a gap in the foothills of the Blue Ridge Mountains, within sight of the Peaks of Otter. As snow fell, the party dug a large square pit six feet deep, lined it with flat stones, placed the gold and silver filled pots on the stones, and covered everything up with dirt, rocks and forest debris.

Beale then went back 2,000 miles to the mining site. Later, he repeated his long trek east with another load of the precious metals. This was buried at or near the original site in November 1821.

This part of his task completed, Beale, with the help of one or more of his partners, next devised an elaborate system of incredible complex codes, which, when broken, would reveal where the treasure had been buried. They covered three sheets of paper with long series of numerals. Cipher number one tells how to find the hidden pots of gold, silver and jewels. Cipher number two describes the complete contents of the treasure vault, and the third one lists the names of the 30 men who were to divide the contents equally.

When this was done, the codes were carefully placed in a metal strongbox, fastened with a tough lock. The nine men who had buried the ore, agreed to leave the box with Robert Morris, innkeeper at the old Washington Hotel in Lynchburg — a man they all kenw and trusted. They stayed at the hotel for a few days, then left again for the west to continue their mining.

Morris never was to see Beale or any of the other men again. The mystique was beginning. Two months after the adventurers had left Virginia, Morris did get a curious letter from Beale posted from St. Louis, then a small hunting and trading post on the western frontier. It said the papers in the strongbox would be meaningless without the proper decoding keys. These keys, Beale stated, were in a sealed envelope that had been given to a friend in St. Louis with instructions to mail it to Morris in June 1832 — ten years later — if by then the band of 30 men had not returned themselves to claim the money.

Morris hid the box under some clutter in an old shed adjacent to the hotel. The ten years passed, and not only had no one from Beale's party come back, but there was no letter from St. Louis. Yet, incredibly, Morris had forgotten about the box. It was not until 1845 — 23 years later — that Morris stumbled upon the strongbox while searching for a harness in the shed. He had the lock broken and opened it. Inside were some old receipts, a couple of letters, and the three coded sheets of numbers. One of the letters, from Beale, told the details of their western expedition, how they found the gold, and how, and in general terms, where, they had buried it.

Morris tried to decipher the codes, but, as have thousands of others since, found them too difficult. Again, inexplicably, he set the box aside. Seventeen years later, a year before he died, Morris, by then reasonably sure that no one was going to return, handed the box and its contents over to James Ward, a trusted family friend. Driven more by curiosity than greed, for he was a man of "independent means," Ward worked day and night on the intriguing codes. Purely by accident he discovered that the second code was keyed to words in the U. S. Declaration of Independence. Laboriously, he deciphered it. It read: "I have deposited in the county of Bedford about four miles from Buford's Inn in an excavation or vault six feet below the surface of the ground the following articles belonging to the parties whose names are given in number three (the third coded sheet) herewith. The first deposit was ten hundred and 14 pounds of gold and thirty-eight hundred pounds of silver. This was deposited November 1819. The second deposit was made December 1821, and consisted of nineteen hundred and seven pounds of gold and twelve hundred and 88 pounds of silver. Also jewels obtained in St. Louis . . . The above is packed securely in iron pots with iron covers. The vault is lined with stones and the vessels lie on solid rock and are covered with other stones. Paper number one describes the exact location of the vault so no difficulty will be had in finding it."

Ward then worked feverously on the two remaining unbroken codes . . . "till his determination and his family fortune ran out." Finally, in 1885, he gave up and published the "Beale Papers" which included copies of everything that had been found in the box, as well as the deciphered code number two and an account of his own efforts to break the other two. He also issued a warning, which has turned out to be excellent advice that has rarely, if ever, been heeded. He said, "devote only such time as can be spared to the task, and if you can spare no time, let the matter alone."

The Beale Papers spread across Virginia like wildfire, and from that time on, for well over 100 years, vast hordes of fortune seekers have descended on rural Bedford County to search for the lost gold and silver. Literal armies of crytographers, computer programmers, historians, professional treasure hunters, and just plain common folks, from all over, have tried to decipher the codes, running the numbers through thousands of books, documents and other papers that were published before 1822. And thousands of tons of Bedford dirt have been dug and redug all across the county. Even with all the tools of modern technology — the most advanced computers, the most sophisticated metal detectors, and the powerful arms of back-hoes and the blades of bulldozers — nothing, not even a minute nugget, has been found. Ironically, small fortunes have been lost in the insatiable search that has yet to be quenched.

Millions of words have been written about the Beale treasure, thousands of maps have been drawn up, and countless teams of experts, including one called the Beale Cypher Association, have been formed — but all efforts have been in vain. The rich cache, if it exists, remains as safe in the ground today as it did the day Beale and his team buried it.

There are many who believe the treasure is one of the most elaborate and cruel hoaxes ever devised. But for everyone who doubts its existence, there are ten who will not let go of the dream of a lifetime. The hunt goes on. Each spring and summer new or renewed hope blossoms and yet more people come to Bedford to try their hand as others work incessantly into the wee hours of the mornings at home trying to break the maddening codes.

Is the treasure real? Will the codes ever be denuded and the grand prize found? To long-time Bedford County residents, such questions seem almost academic today. Many of them are convinced the ghost of Thomas Jefferson Beale hangs close in the vacant valleys between the mountains somewhere out near the vicinity of Buford's Inn, either laughing or crying, as a haunting reminder to the foibles and frustrations of his fellow man in the eternal quest for fame and fortune.

A Legion of Lexington Lore

exington! Land of Lee and Jackson. History, Tradition, Natural beauty. The Valley. The Blue Ridge Mountains.

There are many, many old manor houses in Lexington and the surrounding area of Rockbridge County which harbor their share of resident ghosts. One might think, since their homes, colleges, churches and final resting places are here, that stories of the spiritual return of the two great and revered Confederate military leaders, Robert E. Lee, and Thomas "Stonewall" Jackson, might surface, but such is not the case. There are however, several interesting tales which have been extracted from personal interviews, the Roanoke Times and the Rockbridge County News, Curio Magazine, the files of The Rockbridge Historical Society, William Henry Foote's "Sketches of Virginia," "the History of Rockbridge County," and Anne McCorkle Knox' book, "The Gentle Ghosts." Following is a sampling:

* * * * *

THE REPEATING GUNSHOTS

est of town, on Route 60 heading toward Dark Hollow, is a frame house which has been added on to an original black log cabin believed to have been built before the Revolutionary War started in 1775. The battered old stone chimney, once the dominant feature of the house, has long appeared as if it would crumble in the teeth of even a moderate wind. Yet it has withstood the years because it was contructed to sway with the breeze.

Sometime early this century there was a zoo attached to the house, complete with a monkey and other animals. One night, at about nine p.m., the house owner got into a violent argument with a guest, lost his temper completely, pulled out his "old fashioned pistol," and fired three times, killing the guest.

As the years passed, Harvey Muterspaw and his family moved into the house, and on each anniversary of the shooting, three distinct and loud shots would be heard, and the flashes of pistol fire could be seen. They always occurred at nine p.m., and always in front of the big fireplace (where the murder took place.) The annual firings are followed by stony silence.

"I never did believe in ghosts," says Kathleen Black, Harvey Muterpaw's daughter, who lived in the house as a young girl. "But I did hear those noises. I've heard the shots, and I've heard people talking when there was no one there." she adds. Her father, who died in 1971, also heard the shots several times over the years, but they never seemed to disturb him. "They don't bother me none," he once said. "The ghosts let me alone, and I don't bother the ghosts!'

* * * * *

MRS. TRENNIS' HIDDEN TREASURE

No one knew where she came from or who she was. Some suggested she was a witch who possessed occult powers. Her name was Mrs. Trennis and she kept mostly to herself. She eked out what most neighbors assumed was a meagre living by selling cider and ginger cakes, both to local residents and to those passing through the area on stage coaches. And she lived, rent free, in an old previously-deserted building in Springfield.

Day by day and year by year, the haggish old woman began building a sizeable collection of gold, silver and copper coins from her sales of refreshments. It was said she squirreled her horde away in an old brass kettle which she hid under a loose board in her kitchen-bedroom. In time, Mrs. Trennis grew old and became bedridden. She was cared for by a 10-year-old orphan.

One night in the middle of winter, this child saw the old woman get up, pry the floor board loose, lift the kettle full of coins up, and head outside in the early morning darkness. Sometime later, she returned and collapsed on her bed. The next day Mrs. Trennis died.

And from that day on several families moved into the house, and quickly moved out. They said they were terrified by the strange noises heard beneath the floor and in the walls. When no one else would move in, the old house was torn down. Soonafter, one evening a workman said he saw "an old lady" walk briskly up the road as if in a hurry. He said she stopped in front of a wagon, where the house once stood, and then she seemed to "wither like some autumn flower," and vanished under the wagon. The workman searched for her, but found nothing. Oddly, there were no tracks on the dusty roadside, or on the spot where the house used to be.

* * * * *

KEYDET HAUNTS AT VMI

There are still a few oldtimers left in Lexington who will tell you — in absolute sincerity — that they have heard Sir Moses Ezekiel's statue of "Virginia Mourning Her Dead" moan on certain evenings at dusk and that they have seen real tears streaming down the bronze chiseled face. They say that "she" mourns above the graves of six of the seven VMI cadets who died in the battle of New Market during the Civil War. There is, too, an unsubstantiated account of a lone cadet who was locked by accident one night in Jackson Memorial Hall and claimed that he saw the figures in the mural of the same battle moving. He also allegedly heard the sounds and saw the flashes of gunfire. In her book "The Gentle Ghosts," Anne McCorkle Knox said, "and there are other stories, almost too sad and terrible to tell."

A more popular legend, the so-called "Yellow Peril of VMI," is said to have occurred a number of years ago in the haunted third stoop of VMI Barracks, where, incidentally, Major Thomas J. Jackson was quartered when he taught at the school. Supposedly, a "Rat" freshman was ordered to stay in an upper classman's room here one night until the third year man returned. When he did, he found the freshman gone, and when he confronted him, the Rat appeared deeply shaken. He stammered that something was moving under the old floor boards. A search in the crawl space beneath the boards proved futile.

As word of the incident got around, several cadets gathered on the third stoop a few nights later, when the moon was full. They said later that a "hideous yellow face with a bleeding scar" looked in their shadeless window. It was not the face of a mortal being, rather an awful spectral image that appeared to be looking for someone or something. It so frightened several Chinese students attending VMI at the time, that it is said they left school immediately without notifying the authorities, and never returned!

* * * * *

THE MASSACRE OF BALCONY DOWNS

It is known hereabout as the "Massacre of Balcony Downs." It occurred in December 1742 in what is now known as the McDowell Cemetery on Route 11 near Fairfield, the oldest burial place in Borden's Grant, which includes most of Rockbridge County. It was here, at that fateful time, that a troop of 23 Onandaga and Oneida Indians from Pennsylvania were travelling through the county enroute to settle an old score with some other Indians further south. Uneasy settlers in the area decided to attack them, but the wily Redmen laid an ambush and killed militia leader Captain John McDowell and seven of his men. There is no historic account of what the Indians did to the bodies, although a legend began circulating that they were either scalped or beheaded, or both. In his book, "Sketches of Virginia," William Henry Foote quoted some of the surviving settlers as saying they gathered the "bloody corpses on horseback, and laid them side by side, near McDowell's dwelling, while they prepared their graves with overwhelming sorrow."

More than a century and a half later, a Lexington native named John W. Smith was passing through the old cemetery one evening at midnight on horseback when he was 16 years old. Smith, who later was described as "an earnest churchman and an honest man, not given to exaggeration, said he came upon a man walking in the rain and spoke to him not once, but twice. When he received no reply, he looked closer. Smith said, "And then I saw he din't have no head. It just about skeered me to death! It would have skeered anybody." Smith had not been drinking. He didn't drink, and he said it was light enough to see. He added that the person or thing he saw had on a long army overcoat, "and if that man had a head, I couldn't see it. He came out of the cemetery." Smith had seen enough. "I throwed the switch on that old horse and came away from there." He noted that he told others about his eerie experience, but nobody seemed to want to talk about it.

* * * * *

THE BODY AT LIME KILN BRIDGE

t may well be the most notorious murder case in the history of Rockbridge County. It was in March 1920, that the body of young Aubrey Tyree, who had recently returned from serving in the Army in France, was discovered washed up on the bank near "Brown's Hole," between the Lime Kiln Bridge and town. He had been bludgeoned to death and apparently his body was thrown from the bridge into the ice covered waters below.

Subsequent investigation led to the arrest of a farmer named Addison Mohler. Mohler, who lived on his land at the foot of Hogback Mountain, had a long-standing relationship with a much younger woman named Jessie Chaplin. However, when Tyree came home from overseas, he began calling on the girl. And then he mysteriously disappeared one night. His body was found several weeks later, and eventually, a long trail of circumstantial evidence led to the arrest of Mohler. In his house, law officers found "more than suspicious marks of a bloody struggle." Blood stains were discovered, as was a mountain stone with dried blood on it. Then, some neighbors reported that at about the time of the murder they had passed over the Lime Kiln Bridge one evening and had noticed a strange fresh hole in the ice; one they said was large enough for a man's body to pass through.

Over the next three years, Mohler went through four separate trials. In three of them, there were hung juries. During one trial he was found quilty, but he won a reversal on an appeal. Finally, on September 3, 1923, he was set free. One of the first things he did was go back to his farm and board up the so-called "death cabin." It is said he spent the rest of his life in "desolate solitude."

Oldtimers in the area say that when the gray mists rise to hide the clear water beneath Lime Kiln Bridge, the body of young Aubrey Tryee, wrapped in a white shroud, still can be seen floating on top of the moving current. It appears, they believe, as a spectral vision seeking a vengeance never fulfilled on earth.

CHAPTER 26

Scary Scenes at Stonewall Cottage

(Author's note: I am indebted to attorney Joseph B. Yount III of Waynesboro, who wrote a paper in 1979 about his family and its associated history with Stonewall Cottage in Rockingham County, and was gracious enough to share a copy of it with me. the paper is titled "Ghosts and Frights at Stonewall Cottage," and Mr. Yount says, "All of these events happened before I was born. I have done my best to recount them exactly as they were often told me by my late father, Joseph Bryon Yount, Jr. I have tried not to exaggerate . . . I have tried to be as accurate as possible. some of my kinsmen may think it ridiculous to record these stories. In doing so I do not intend to dishonor the dead . . . The various stories about Stonewall Cottage and its haunts . . . have been a part of my family folklore all my life. Truth is stranger than fiction, they say, and I have no reason to believe that any of this is untrue.")

Some downright scary things have happened over the years at Stonewall Cottage on the Valley turnpike just north of Harrisonburg. Some of the occurrences remain inexplicable and are linked with the supernatural, while others have been caused by quite natural and rational, if unusual, means. Yet the effect has been much the same — spine-tingling chills!

Take the case of the reburial of Uncle Joseph Dovel, for example. This, "ghostly excitement at Stonewall Cottage is not really extra-terrestial, but must have been equally hair-raising," writes Yount. It seems that in 1938, several family graves were to be moved from the land at Stonewall Cottage to lots in Woodbine Cemetery at Harrisonburg. Among those to be moved was Captain Joseph M.

Dovel, "the young lawyer who had joined the Confederate Army and become a captain of the celebrated Valley Rangers of the Stonewall Brigade, only to become injured and ill with camp fever and return home to die in 1863 at age 23." The undertaker hired a crew of black laborers to exhume the bodies. They found Captain Dovel buried in a cast iron, bullet-shaped coffin with a glass window over his face. The hinged coffin was held shut by two large bolts.

"Aunt Bettie Post and my father were present when the iron casket was raised. The men dusted off the window, and there was Captain Dovel, looking as if he were merely asleep," says Yount. "He was buried in his Confederate uniform, with a crimson sash for decoration. Aunt Bettie asked the undertaker if he would open the casket for a moment, to enable her to see her uncle 'in full regalia.' The men unscrewed the screws and lifted the top." As soon as the air hit inside, there was a mild, soundless implosion. The body disintegrated instantly into dust before their eyes. Yount adds that some of the Blacks ran off in all directions, Aunt Bettie rushed back to the house, "and my father had yet another terrifying time at Stonewall Cottage to remember."

Yount's father was the sole witness to another of the "colorful after effects" of the haunted stories that circulated about the cottage. This occurred in 1934, when Aunt Laura died sitting up in her chair one night. She had apparently suffered a fatal attack during the evening, before coming upstairs to bed, and her body was not discovered until the next morning. Aunt Laura had left instructions that she wanted to be buried in a shroud, and this request proved to be somewhat difficult to fulfill. Yount's father went from store to store in Harrisonburg "trying to locate the old-fashioned, long out-of-date garment. He could not find one, and one of the neighbors commissioned a nearby Mennonite lady to make one.

"The undertaker had prepared the body in the coffin and placed it, as was the custom, in the front parlor. The house was dark, the shutters still closed in the front, seldom-used rooms. My father went around to the rear where the family and friends were gathered. After a while, Aunt Sallie asked my father to go over to the parlor to get her something from behind the organ. He had to pass through several rooms and the hall to get to the parlor. It had been the aunts' custom to carry keys and lock the doors behind them as they went from room to room at Stonewall Cottage.

"My father always said he wasn't afraid of anyone living, but didn't like to fool with the dead. Nervously, he entered the parlor... (he) glanced at Aunt Laura, her eyes closed, her form lying stiffly in

Stonewall Cottage – 1895. Left to right, Laura Belle Stephens, 1862-1934; Martha Josephine Stephens, 1856-1899; Mary Elizabeth Dovel Stephens, 1829-1902; Sallie Georgiana Stephens, 1870-1938.

the coffin. He walked past to the end of the room and reached behind the organ. Suddenly, he heard a loud snap, which he always described as sounding like a 'rat' trap going off. He looked around and saw Aunt Laura in the coffin, her eyes opened and apparently staring at him, her head turned in his direction, her false teeth half out of her opened mouth.

"My father claimed he was so much in shock that it took what seemed an hour for him to walk past the coffin and leave the parlor. He called out the front door to the undertaker, who came immediately. What had happened? Because of the delay in discovering the body, staying as it was in a sitting position all night long, rigor mortis had set in. The undertaker had braced her mouth shut with a brace under her chin, obscured by the high collar of the shroud. My father apparently jarred it loose as he walked across the creaky floor. The brace slipped, throwing the head ajar . . . My mother remembered well how white and pale he looked when he returned to the Stonewall Cottage kitchen."

Yount says one of the unexplained psychic manifestations concerned an old lady who always sat by the fireplace smoking a clay pipe. "After her death, others in the house could still hear her knocking out her clay pipe against the fireplace after everyone else had gone to bed for the night. This story, often told me by my father, is verified by his sisters, who are still living today (1979). They all said without question that the lady knocking out her pipe was Martha Burnsides Stevens Cowan (1806-1895)." Yount says, however, he is not sure whether this phenomena actually took place at Stonewall Cottage or at a house near Lacey Springs, five or six miles to the north.

Under a heading called "Restless Spirits That Wander," Yount writes: "I now come to what I believe to be the 'true' ghost story of Stonewall Cottage. It happened in 1902. For its accururacy I have virtually identical oral accounts from two people, namely (1) my father, who was five and 1/2 years old at the time and present at the occasion, and (2) his first cousin, Addie Yount Wood, who was 15 years old at the time . . . Addie was a favorite niece of my grandfather, Joseph B. Yount, who also witnessed the events of 1902. She lived on a farm near Waynesboro, Virginia, neighboring his, and she well remembers the excitement caused when he came home from Stonewall Cottage in 1902 and related this story. She says he told it to her many times, and, as she puts it, 'I know that Uncle Joe wouldn't have made up something like that.'

"(I might add that my father's younger sisters have tended to discredit the story. Even while he was living, they tended to discredit it as largely the account of an exaggerating imagination. It seems to embarrass them to think abour their grandmother as a ghostly presence. My father always cut them short when they talked that way, insisting that he knew what he had seen. My father was a colorful, educated man, an active practicing attorney for 47 years; he had a keen memory and could imitate voices of long-dead people; he loved to tell stories of old timers. I have no reason whatsoever to believe that he fabricated any part of this story, especially since his account agreed in virtually every detail with what Addie Wood remembers her Uncle Joe telling her in 1902.)

"Stonewall Cottage in 1902 was the home of Mary Dovel Stephens, 72, and her two daughters, Laura, 40, and Sallie, 32. . . Brother Will, who had disappointed the family by his marked lack of responsibility and unwillingness to take over the farm operation, was living in Winchester, Virginia. . . The Stephens family of Stonewall Cottage was well-to-do, but it was very burdensome work for the three women to operate the big farm with often undependable hired farm labor.

"One late summer day in 1902, Mary Dovel Stephens, while eating a hearty dinner, remarked to her daughters that there was some very important business that she needed to tend to at once. (Some speculated that she intended to write a will that would eliminate her son from sharing in any part of her share of the farm.). . .Immediately after the dinner at which she had made these remarks, Mary Dovel Stephens lay down to rest on a fainting couch and without warning died instantly of an apparent heart attack. She was buried in the family cemetery south of the house near the orchard. A week of so after the funeral, Sallie and Laura asked their brother-in-law, Joseph B. Yount, to come to Stonewall Cottage for several days to help them with business affairs in connection with the settlement of the estate. Joe brought his 5 1/2-year-old son, Byron, my father, along with him.

"The first night of their visit, Joe and his young son went to bed in the front upstairs bedroom, a room in which an old rocking chair was located. Sallie and Laura were supposedly asleep in the upstairs bedrooms to the rear of the house. Shortly after they went to bed, Joe and his son heard the distinct sound of the front door being opened and the tread of footsteps lightly ascending the main stairs. Suddenly, the door to their bedroom seemed to blow open, and the rocking chair began to rock as if some ghostly figure were sitting in it. Grandfather attributed these strange happenings to the wind, arose from bed, and closed the door. He and his son fell asleep. When they awoke, the bedroom door was open again, with no indication that it had been opened by anyone else in the house.

"Grandfather said nothing, not wanting to alarm the recently-bereaved sisters-in-law. The next night, perhaps out of caution, he pulled a side chair against the inside of the bedroom door to insure that the wind could not blow it open. He and his son were nearly asleep when, again, they heard the front door open and close, the sound of footsteps ascending the stairs, and then, to their amazement, the door was pushed open, as if by some invisible force, sliding the side chair back against the wall, and then the rocking chair began to rock.

"This was too much for my grandfather. He abruptly arose, hurriedly dressed, took my father by the hand, and walked down to the rear of the house, where Sallie and Laura were supposed to be sleeping. To his surprise, he found them both awake, each with a frightened look. The expression on his face caused them to say, 'Well, you have heard it, too! It has happened every night since mother was buried. We thought we were losing our minds. If it continues, we will have to move away from here.'

"The next day my grandfather took Sallie and Laura to see their minister and told him of the apparent poltergeist. He was the minister who served the nearby Melrose Church of the Brethren, where the dead woman had also belonged. He contacted one or two fellow pastors . . . That night at Stonewall Cottage the ministers joined Sallie and Laura, my grandfather and father, for prayers. The ministers read appropriate words from the Bible and led the group in prayer. I have never looked in the Bible for the text, but my father described it as some verse about 'restless spirits who wander' or 'troubled spirits who wander.'

"The prayers and readings were enough to summons the spirit, and the mysterious footsteps were soon heard. They then conducted further prayers, and one of the ministers exhorted the spirit, 'In the name of God, what do you want?' These words were repeated, and when there was no response the ministers then said, 'In the name of God, be at rest.' The prayers and exhortations were effective. Never again during the remaining 36 years of family occupancy did the restless spirit wander the halls of Stonewall Cottage.

"My father always professed to believe that it had been the ghost of Mary Dovel Stephens, who had died before attending to her important business and who could not rest. . . . All I can promise the readers of this account is that I have not exaggerated it one iota. I have written it as it was told to me by one who was there."

The Psychically Sensitive Siblings

t is not rare for a ghost or ghosts to appear or make their presence known to more than one member of a family. Although some spirits have been seen or felt by just one member, it is just as common for two or more persons in a house, even a generation or more apart, to experience the same phenomena. It is rare when two members of the same family experience two different sets of manifestations — at two different houses! Such was the case, nearly two centuries ago, involving brothers — Colonel John Cabell of Buckingham County, and Colonel Samuel Cabell who resided in Nelson County. Each had a singular encounter under entirely different circumstances. A probable answer is that each was somewhat psychic although neither was likely aware of it at the time.

John Cabell lived in a house called Green Hill, built in 1762 of heart pine. He was a man of considerable stature in Buckingham County and served as sheriff, as a delegate to the Convention of Williamsburg, and as a representative in the General Assembly of Virginia. He was also known to be a man of a fiery temper and a cast iron will.

In his younger days, John was not a religious man, however, But he became a convert in a highly dramatic fashion one night while he sat in Green Hill's parlor alone, possibly shortly after the death of his second wife right after the turn of the 19th century. As he repined before a hearty log fire, the great hall upon which the parlor opened to suddenly filled with what has been described as "an unearthly wind." John then gasped as he saw three female figures standing by a large table. On the table was the family Bible, and the pages began turning rapidly "although no hand touched it." Understandably, the Colonel took this as a serious omen for him to study the Holy Book, which he did from that day on, becoming a devout believer.

Some years after his death in 1815, some family members and friends were in the house partaking in a session of "table rappings" — a form of entertainment preceding the Ouija board in which spirits of the past were called forth. John's name was called again and again, but no response was forthcoming. Frustrated at the inactivity, one person exclaimed, "Oh, he was a hot tempered, contrary man when living and he is the same man when dead." At the very moment of the utterance of this slight, according to the witnesses, the large mahogany table with a heavy marble top "rose up bodily in the air and crashed down again." The table rapping participants scattered to all corners of the house and never played the game again!

On another occasion, as a visitor sat in the sitting room with family members, "laughing and talking," the bar across the front door was flung aside and the door burst open. And this was no ordinary door. It had been not only locked, but also barred with heavy wooden timbers held in place by iron hooks. When no one was found in the area, someone remarked, "Something must have displeased John" In addition, there were constant rappings heard in different parts of Green Hill over the years, which everyone interpreted as evidence that the Colonel was still looking after his earthly possessions long after he had departed to the spirit world. His vigil continued for some time, because even after the family sold the house, the new owner became so terrified of such actions as having his clothes yanked off his bed, he refused to sleep in that particular bedroom alone.

* * * * *

With brother Samuel, though, the manifestations took a different form. He had been a "gallant soldier" throughout the Revolutionary War, and took up residence in a new home in Nelson County in 1785. It was called Soldier's Joy. It was a pleasant, two story frame house perfumed each springtime by the sweet scent of locust blossoms.

Samuel settled into a comfortable, bucolic life which ended abruptly one stormy night when a loud pounding on the front door awakened the household. A servant answered, and in a strode a "repulsive looking peddlar," dripping wet from the driving rain, who demanded lodging for the evening. Samuel declined at first, owing to the man's forbidding countenance." But the peddlar was loudly insistent, almost threatening, and the rain was pouring down in torrents. Finally, the host relented, gave the man food, and put him up in a room in the far wing.

At about one in the morning, Colonel Cabell awoke suddenly, and was horrified to see the evil-faced peddlar standing over him holding a long sharp knife at arm's length, ready to strike. Instinctively, Samuel struck a blow with such "terrific force," that it sent the peddlar reeling backwards. His head hit hard against the sharp edge of a heavy old wardrobe, and he collapsed on the floor, blood streaming from a deep cut. Samuel called the servants and when they examined the man, he was dead.

A descendent of the Colonel said, generations later, that the stain "has never left the floor." And it has been sworn to, by a number of witnesses, that on certain nights, at exactly one in the morning, the sound of a dull heavy thud — as of a body falling — has been heard at the spot of the bloodstain that will not go away!

The Spectral Hound of the Blue Ridge

ook out. It's coming!'

"There was a thin, crisp, continuous patter from somewhere in the heart of that crawling bank. The cloud was within 50 yards of where we lay, and we stared at it, all three, uncertain what horror was about to break from the heart of it. I was at Holme's elbow, and I glanced for an instant at his face. It was pale and exultant, his eyes shining brightly in the moonlight. But suddenly they started forward in a rigid, fixed stare, and his lips parted in amazement. At the same instant Lestrade gave a yell of terror and threw himself face downwards upon the ground.

"I sprang to my feet, my inert hand grasping my pistol, my mind paralyzed by the dreadful shape which had sprung out upon us from the shadows of the fog. A hound it was, an enormous coal-black hound, but not such a hound as mortal eyes have ever seen. Fire burst from its open mouth, its eyes glowed with a smoldering glare, its muzzle and hackles dewlap were outlined in flickering flame.

"Never in the delirious dream of a disordered brain could anything more savage, more appalling, more hellish be conceived than that dark form and savage face which broke upon us out of the wall of fog.

"With long bounds the huge black creature was leaping down the track, following hard upon the footsteps of our friend. So paralyzed were we by the apparition that we allowed him to pass before we had recovered our nerve. . . . . Far away on the path we saw Sir Henry looking back, his face white in the moonlight, his hands raised in horror, glaring helplessly at the frightful thing which was hunting him down. . . . ."

This is how, nearly 100 years ago, Sir Arthur Conan Doyle

described the great black beast — "gaunt, savage, and as large as a small lioness" — in his classic Sherlock Holmes' thriller, "The Hound of the Baskervilles." In this story the crime is built around a legend which holds that a gigantic hound appeared on the moors before the death of a member of the Baskerville family. However, says Daniel Cohen, author of "The Encyclopedia of Ghosts," "though this was entirely fiction, it was based on an ancient and widespread spectral hound tradition in England."

As an example, Cohen documents a case where a Scottish family experienced just such a phenomenon. The father did not believe in the long-standing tradition, but nevertheless did not tell his wife about it for fear of frightening her. Then one of his children fell ill with smallpox. Though it seemed to be a relatively mild attack, smallpox at the time was a dangerous disease, and the family was quite worried.

One evening, as the family sat down to dinner, the mother went upstairs to check on the sick child. A moment later she came running down the stairs in an excited state. She told her husband that the child was asleep but that there was a large black dog lying on the bed. She exhorted him to chase the dog out of the house. The father knew instantly what the appearance of the dog meant. Filled with fear, he rushed upstairs. There was no dog in sight, and the child was dead.

Other stories of spectral hounds abound. It was said that a small white dog appeared at the gates of the notorious Newgate Prison in the United Kingdom before every execution.

(Author's note: In my book, "The Ghosts of Fredericksburg," I reported on ghost dogs in the Northern Neck of Virginia. One surviving legend involved the periodic sightings — generally in creek pond "bottoms" from which mists often arose above the marshes — of a headless dog. It seemed to roam mostly in the lower section of the Neck, and was occasionally joined by a "white mule . . . a headless man . . . and another dog, this one with a head featuring glowing red eyes." Scores of witnesses reported seeing this dog and their descriptions all were remarkably similar. The animal was as large as a calf, brown in color with patches of gray around his mouth. A large chain encircled its neck and dragged on the ground and rattled as the dog moved. And it moved only at night and only in a certain area between Cockrell's Neck and Heathsville.

Lastly, according to the long-held legend, it only was sighted just before or after the death of a local resident.)

All of the above serves as an eerie prelude to the following account of a massive black spectral dog which, in the late 17th century, was reported to have roamed along Skyline Drive, southwest of Charlottesville. The spectacle was recorded by a Mrs. R. F. Herrick in the Journal of American Folklore, published in 1907. Following are excerpts from that account:

"In Botetourt County, Virginia, there is a pass that was much travelled by people going to Bedford County and by visitors to mineral springs in the vicinity. In the year 1683 the report was spread that at the wildest part of the trail in this pass there appeared at sunset a great black dog, who, with majestic tread, walked in a listening attitude about 200 feet and then turned and walked back. Thus he passed back and forth like a sentinel on guard, always appearing at sunset to keep his nightly vigil and disappearing again at dawn. And so the whispering went with bated breath from one to another, until it had travelled from one end of the state to the other. Parties of young cavaliers were made up to watch for the black dog. Many saw him. Some believed him to be a veritable dog sent by some master to watch; others believed him to be a witch dog.

"A party decided to go through the pass at night, well armed, to see if the dog would molest them. Choosing a night when the moon was full,they mounted good horses and sallied forth. Each saw a great dog larger than any dog they had ever seen, and, clapping spurs to their horses, they rode forward. But they had not calculated

on the fear of their steeds. When they approached the dog, the horses snorted with fear, and in spite of whip, spur, and rein, gave him a wide berth, while he marched on a serenely as if no one were near. The party were (sic) unable to force their horses to take the pass again until after daylight. They were laughed at by their comrades to whom they told their experiences.

"Thereupon they decided to lie in ambush, kill the dog, and bring in his hide. The next night found the young men well hidden behind rocks and bushes with guns in hand. As the last ray of the sunlight kissed the highest peak of the Blue Ridge, the black dog appeared at the lower end of his walk, seemingly unconscious of the presence of the hunter. Again and again they fired and still the dog walked his beat. And fear caught the hearts of the hunters, and they fled wildly away to their companions, and the black dog held the pass at night unmolested.

"Time passed, and year after year went by, until seven years had come and gone, when a beautiful woman came over from the old country, trying to find her husband who eight years before had come to make a home for her in the new land. She traced him to Bedford County and from there all trace of him was lost. Many remembered the tall, handsome man and his dog. Then there came to her ear the tale of the vigil of the great dog of the mountain pass, and she pleaded with the people to take her to see him, saying that if he was her husband's dog he would know her.

"A party was made up and before night they arrived at the gap. The lady dismounted, and walked up to the place where the nightly watch was kept. As the shadows grew long, the party fell back on the trail, leaving the lady alone, and as the sun sank into his purple bed of splendor the great dog appeared. Walking to the lady, he laid his great head in her lap for a moment, then turning, he walked a short way from the trail, looking back to see that she was following. He led her until he paused by a large rock, where he gently scratched the ground, gave a long, low wail, then disappeared.

"The lady called the party to her and asked them to dig. As they had no implements, and she refused to leave, one of them rode back for help. When they dug below the surface they found the skeleton of a man and the hair and bones of a great dog. They found a seal ring on the hand of the man and a heraldic embroidery in silk that the wife recognized. She removed the bones for proper burial and returned to her old home. It was never known who had killed the man. But from that time to this, the great dog, having finished his faithful work, has never appeared again."

CHAPTER 29

The Albino Beasts of Montpelier

(Author's note: In doing research for my book "The Ghosts of Fredericksburg and Nearby Environs," in the winter of 1991, I made inquiries about ghosts at historic Montpelier, the home of James Madison, fourth President of the United States, in Orange County. I was told by authorities of the National Trust for Historic Preservation there, that there were no psychic manifestations to speak of. I thought it a shame at the time, because I love to intertwine Virginia history with supernatural lore wherever possible, such as at Stratford Hall, Robert E. Lee's birthplace in the Northern Neck; at Scotchtown, Patrick Henry's home near Ashland; at Shirley Plantation, home of the Carter family for nine generations, on Route 5 between Richmond and Williamsburg; and many others. But I don't force things. If there are no reports of psychic activity, I accept the fact and move on.

And so, I was especially delighted, in doing the research for this book, to find a gentleman who grew up near the grounds at Montpelier and shared with me not only the spectral experiences his grandparents and distant cousins had there two generations ago, but also related a scary encounter he had in the same area about 25 years ago. I was delighted for three reasons. One, Montpelier is such a rich historic national treasure, it was a great pleasure in itself just to visit it. Two, what was told to me is rather unusual in nature, even when one considers virtually everything in this book is a little unusual. And three, the Madison mansion actually is closer to Charlottesville than Fredericksburg anyway.)

ames Madison, born in King George County, is, of course, known as the father of the U. S. Constitution. He moved to Montpelier as a young child and it was his home for 76 years. Small in physical stature — he was barely over five feet tall — Madison was a brilliant intellectual who dedicated 53 years of his life to public service. He was, among other things: a delegate to the Continental Congress; a member of the Virginia House of Delegates; a U. S. congressman; Secretary of State to Thomas Jefferson; and a two-term U.S. President. In addition to his work on the Constitution, he was one of the authors of the Federalist Papers and was instrumental in negotiating passage of the Bill of Rights. That's quite a resume, exceeded possibly only by his neighbor at Monticello.

The core of Montpelier was built by Madison's father in 1755. The future President himself remodeled and enlarged the house, adding a Tuscan portico in 1797-1800, and making additional changes in the years 1809-1812, including a neoclassical domed garden temple. Today, Montpelier is a 55-room mansion amidst the magnificent grandeur of a 2,700 acre estate. The mansion is surrounded by over 100 other structures, including stables and a bowling alley.

In 1794, Aaron Burr introduced the 43-year-old bachelor Madison to beautiful Dolley Payne Todd, a 26-year-old widow, and they were married soon after. The distinguished couple retired to Montpelier in 1817, after Madison's second term as president was completed. They are buried on the grounds in the family cemetery. Following her husband's death in 1836, Dolley sold the estate in 1844, and it changed hands many times over the next half century.

In 1901, William du Pont, Sr., purchased the property and made "vast alterations." The mansion was enlarged and additional barns, greenhouses, staff houses, a saw mill, blacksmith shop, dairy and train station were built. Mrs. du Pont created a two and a half acre formal garden, and the du Pont's daughter, Marion du Pont Scott, who inherited the estate, added a steeplechase course and initiated the Montpelier Hunt Races, still held the first weekend each November. The National Trust for Historic preservation acquired Montpelier following her death in 1984.

It was during the early tenure of the du Pont's that the ethereal manifestations first occurred according to Lou Southard, an employee of the Virginia State Forestry Service, who grew up in the area. "Actually," says Lou, "family accounts of such phenomena precede the occurrences at Montpelier. I can remember, for example, hearing about my great grandfather's experiences in the late 19th century. Once he was walking past what was said to be a haunted graveyard in the Liberty Mills Bridge area late one night when he was chased by ghosts. He had been a ball player, and he stopped and picked up some rocks and threw them at his pursuers. He said they went right through them. That was enough for him, he ran as fast as he could over the bridge, and lost them. Ghosts won't cross water."

Lou says his grandfather and grandmother, Loney and Nora Southard, both worked at the du Pont estate in the early 20th century. "He fired the furnace at the main house," Lou says. "And they began courting. It must have been sometime around 1915, 1916. Anyway, they would meet in the evenings at the old ice house built by Dolley Madison. They would just sit there, in the cool breeze and talk. Well, one night they were sitting there when they saw something strange emerge out of the woods and walk across the great lawn of the estate. They were astonished at the sight. My grandfather described it as a huge, four-footed animal that was pure white and about the size and with the appearance of a 'small polar bear.' It moved past them toward the house. They got up and followed it across the lawn, at a discretionary distance. They said when it got to a horseshoe hedge, it disappeared before their eyes. Now, my grandparents were not given to unnecessary exaggeration. They swore that's what they saw, and they had no explanation for its mysterious disappearance.

"There is a sort of confirmation to their experience," Lou continues. "I had two distant cousins, who were out horseback riding on the Montpelier grounds one day during that same period, their names were Jack and Claude. Jack was blind. They said that they were riding in the area near the ice house when Jack suddenly asked Claude, what was that between them. Claude looked down and said it appeared to be a large, snow-white animal, which he took to be a calf. They said that whatever it was, it didn't disturb the horses, and that if they speeded up, 'it' speeded up, and if they slowed down, 'it' did so, too. When they reached the bottom of the hill — near the exact spot where my grandparents had seen their 'bear,' they said it vanished. Claude couldn't see it anymore, and Jack couldn't sense its presence anymore. It must have been an exceptionally large animal because they weren't riding ordinary riding horses. They were on work horses. They're about the size of Clydesdales!"

Lou Southard has a possible theory explaining the albino apparition. "Back during those days the du Ponts had a gigantic guard dog which roamed the grounds at night. I think they called it Dickie. It was said to be vicious. It could have been a Mastiff or a St. Bernard or something. I don't know, except that everyone says it was the largest dog they had ever seen. One night the dog apparently tried to jump over a fence, got hung up in it and choked to death on its collar. I have always wondered if the ghost of that dog might have been the large animal my grandparents and cousins reported seeing."

There is a footnote to this story, which Lou says happened to him more than 40 years after the reported sightings. "I grew up there. As a boy I roamed the woods regularly, and I knew every dog within miles. I must have about 12 or 13 when this happened. I had been fishing, and I was walking through a spit of woods that separates the estate from the road. It was just about dusk. I heard the most God-awful howl that anyone could imagine. You could equate it to that of the Hound of the Baskervilles. I mean it was terrorizing. I felt the hair on the back of my neck stand straight up. I started walking faster. And whatever it was that made that horrible noise apparently was keeping pace, because every now and then it would let out another howl. I started running. And then it dawned on me. I was running right toward the same spot in the woods that my grandparents had seen their beast come out of. And it was near where my cousins had been riding. If I kept going in the same direction, I would be right in the area where the ice house was. There was another awful howl and it sounded real close," Lou says. "So I quickly turned the other way and ran through the creek. I didn't stop until I got home.

"I'll tell you, I don't know what was making that noise, because I never saw it. I didn't want to see it. But to this day, whenever I talk about it or even think about it, the hair on the back of my neck still rises!"

Miss Minnie Finds
Peace at Last

(Authors note: Shortly after my book, "The Ghosts of Richmond," was published in 1985, I got a nice letter from Mrs. Diane Carr of Montpelier (the town in Hanover County, not the Madison home in Orange County). She wrote to tell me of the sprightly ghost that she and her husband, Claude, had experienced in the 100-year-old house they had moved into in 1984. Mrs. Carr said she not only believed the "lady" she shared her home with was friendly, but that she also, on one occasion at least, had possibly prevented Mrs. Carr's son from having a serious accident. The following are excerpts from her letter, and a few comments from a conversation with her husband.)

ear Mr. Taylor: First, your book on ghosts in the Richmond area is delightful and informative." (Author's note: how could I leave *that* out!) "Two years ago we moved into a century old farmhouse. We soon learned that we were living in 'Miss Minnie's House.' The owner, until fairly recent times was an old maid who used it as a summer or vacation home. She was from the area, but had a house in Richmond. . . she had a male friend for 30 years but never married him . . . and she must have loved dogs because there are engraved granite tombstones for two of her dogs in the yard.

"I sincerely believe Miss Minnie is still here. To my knowledge there is no tragedy involved. My theory is that she loved the place - enough to keep an interested eye on it. When we came, the house had fallen into disrepair and we set out to restore it to its earlier appearance. Needless to say, it definitely looked worse before it began to look better. We soon heard a man and a woman murmuring to each other."

At this point, Claude Carr picks up the story. "This didn't occur in the house," he says. "It happened outside. I was out by an open shed one day doing some work. I guess it was around mid-day. All of a sudden I heard a woman's voice say, as plain as day, 'I'm hungry.' She said it a couple of times. I thought for sure that Diane had driven home from her job for lunch. But she hadn't said anything that morning about it, so I was kind of surprised to hear her. Except when I looked around, she wasn't there. No one was there! I don't know where the sound came from, but I know I heard it."

Mrs. Carr continues with her letter: "Several times when I was home alone I had a feeling she was there - although there was no obvious evidence. Sort of the feeling you have as a child when you can feel your mother is in the house, although you don't really see or hear her. As the house became more liveable she seemed to grow more content.

"She can open doors. This could be attributed to the age of the house if it were just the interior doors. But she can open the back door even though it has a new deadbolt lock. The worse thing she has done was grab my foot and give it a good yank one night while I was in bed. Luckily, that must not have been fun and hasn't been repeated. The latest 'thing' is the sound of a music box playing very faintly from the room we believe was hers.

"I believe it's possible that she can leave the house. About two miles away is another house about the same age. One day as I drove past it I saw a tall thin woman in white walking alone as if she were checking on her vegetable garden. The shape of her clothes resembled those of the thirties (1930s) or early forties. When I slowed my car for a better look, she had vanished and I realized it was just a big farmer's field planted in some low-growing crop. Now maybe they have a ghost too, but I felt it was Miss Minnie.

"About a month after that our 20-year-old son was coming by the same area in the middle of the night when he said he had the sensation that someone was in the car. Suddenly, all the indicator lights on his dashboard started flashing. He slowed down quickly, and saw just ahead a fallen tree across the road. He felt it was Miss Minnie trying to get him safely home.

"I hope I haven't bored you, but I wanted to introduce you to Miss Minnie."

The Carrs say that things have gotten very quiet in the years since Diane wrote the letter. They believe Miss Minnie has "settled in," and is at ease, sharing her house with them.

CHAPTER 31

A 'Release Ceremony' at Selma

When the magnificent, 20-room, white columned mansion known as Selma was built in 1856, it stood isolated in the center of a 790-acre estate well outside the confines of the town of Staunton. In the nearly century and a half since, the city has grown to more or less "enclose" the three-story Greek Revival home. Yet still it maintains its splendor. Inside are no less than 13 fireplaces, one of which curiously has no opening into a chimney. Handcarved mantels are different in each room, with the most intricate, featuring a Grecian design of Bacchus, God of Wine, in the dining room. The parlor ceiling is vividly painted with cherubs holding garlands, circled by plaster bas-relief flowers, leaves and garlands.

Despite the pleasant surroundings, however, Selma was the scene, during the Civil War, of a dark tragedy which, until 1982, cast an unhappy pall over the environs. It seems that in the last stages of the war a young Confederate soldier was chased into the house by a Union trooper and was killed at the dining room mantel, where his blood stained the floor, allegedly for years. For the next 120 years, the slain Reb's spirit remained in the house, confused and perhaps angered, roaming about in the attic, on the stairs and elsewhere. One well published account of his presence was said to have taken place in 1872 when the property was then owned by the Williams family of South Carolina.

Several members of the family as well as the servants told others that they often saw the ghost about in the house. On this particular occasion, a visitor at Selma arose from a tea table downstairs to go upstairs, and when she returned she asked her hosts, "Who was the gentleman entering the room as I went out?" She was told that no

one had come in. She then insisted that a "soldier in uniform" had passed her as she went out. The lady had no prior knowledge of what had happened at the mansion. Later, when the H. Arthur Lamb family occupied Selma, the same manifestation appeared. The Confederate would be seen on the stairs, entering the dining room, or standing quietly by the blood-stained hearth "as if he were a member of the family circle!" Once, a new servant asked if she should lay a place at the table for the "gentleman." When she was asked what gentleman, she replied, "Why, the soldier gentleman."

Although ownership of the mansion passed through several hands over the years, the apparitional soldier stayed on. In the early 1900s, when Colonel William Beard of Tallahassee, Florida, bought the place, he had great difficulty getting servants "on account of the ghost." Members of the Beard family said they distinctly heard steps of a "ghostly patrol," night after night, passing and repassing across the rustic bridge on the grounds, but because they wanted to sell the estate they were reluctant to talk about it.

In the mid-1960s, Richard and Claudette Obenschain, the current owners, told of the bizarre incident which happened to a woman overnight guest. She was sleeping in the same room that the soldier's mother apparently once occupied, and in the middle of the night she was unceremoniously shoved out of the bed onto the floor. No one could convince her that it wasn't the spectral soldier who had pushed her.

It wasn't that the young man was mean. Quite the contrary. One writer described him as "polite, attentive, as though listening to the conversation of the family, but not taking part." His image was described as "so clear and distinct that he was often mistaken for a living man, his manner was so calm and casual, his presence so convincing, that residents often accepted him . . ." With the lone exception of the lady who was nudged from her bed, no one really had fear of the soldier.

Everything remained relatively calm at Selma until 1982, when a Blue Ridge Community College parapsychology class visited the house as part of a field trip. One of the 30 members of the class was Phyllis Atwater of Charlottesville, a woman who said she was "very sensitive" to psychic phenomena. She has had past encounters with haunted houses. Once, for example, in Boise, Idaho, she went with a newspaper reporter to a house said to be haunted by a young boy. Manifestations supposedly included doors and windows opening and closing by themselves, and a rocking chair that would float in the air unassisted. During the search, the boy appeared to Mrs. Atwater on a staircase, straddling the family cat. The reporter wrote an article on the experience and on the day the story was published the house burned to the ground!

Another time, beside a fresh grave site in a cemetery outside Roanoke, she saw "what appeared to be a small boy standing downcast and lonely." She conversed with him, asking him why he hadn't gone to the "light," a reference to the intense light claimed to have been seen by many who have been declared clinically dead and were then returned to life. The boy said he had seen the light, but hadn't followed it because his mother told him never to go anywhere without her permission. At Selma, Mrs. Atwater said the landlady told the group they could go anywhere in the house with the exception of the attic. "She was adamant that no one should go up there." As soon as no one was looking, Mrs. Atwater went straight to the attic. "I had to," she said. "The feelings were very strong from that portion of the house. Once her eyes adjusted to the dim light there, she saw a spirit which "had no earthly form, but rather presented a hodgepodge of blotches hanging in mid air. I'd never seen anything like it," she recalled. "I was shocked, but I knew better than to show fear or react emotionally."

The entity then spoke to her, demanding that she go away immediately. She told it she was not there to do harm, merely to help it. "Something was happening I didn't think was possible," she said. "This was a soul that literally was dissipating. All the other energy forms I'd dealt with stayed true to their own coherent structures.

This one was breaking up."

She then went downstairs, and on the way out of the attic met a man and his wife who was blind, headed for the attic. The blind woman said, "You saw it, didn't you?" Mrs. Atwater acknowledged that she had, and then she told the group instructor, David McKnight, that a "release ceremony" must be conducted at once if the spirit of the Confederate was to be saved. At a discussion held by the group, the blind lady, too, said she had felt the presence of the ghost and found it to be "very foreboding and confrontational." After Mrs. Atwater stressed to the landlady the importance of releasing the soldier from an unhappy existence, the release ceremony was set up for that evening. Its purpose, she said, was to contact the spirit and let it know what was happening.

In a subsequent article in the Waynesboro News-Virginian by staff writer Charles Culbertson, Mrs. Atwater told of how she conducted the ceremony. "I counseled it," she stated. I said I understood the circumstances of its death, of the terrible era it had come from, and I told it forcefully that it needed help. I said it must go to the light before it was destroyed. She added that the soldier resisted all the way, and then she had to force it "by dint of will" to leave the house. She said the spirit finally "sighed with resignation" and moved on to the after life it had avoided for 118 years.

At that precise moment, the clock struck midnight.

"The soul is an extension of God, and after death it normally progresses on," Mrs. Atwater said. "But here we had a young man who died traumatically. He was imprisoned in Selma by his own emotions and by the selfishness of others." She noted that she believed the spirit of the soldier was dissipating because "the energy of other people sapped his vital force over the years. "We did the right thing and freed him."

The landlady wasn't so sure. "I liked my ghost," she said. "He made a wonderful conversation piece."

C H A P T E R   3 2

Strange Guests at the 'Ghost Hotel'

air raising noises in the dead of night . . . bone-chilling apparitions and ectoplasmic manifestations". . .all part of a "spectral vortex". . . at Augusta County's "Ghost Hotel." This is how Waynesboro News-Virginian reporter Charles Culbertson described the 240-year-old brick mansion west of Staunton owned by Bill and Marie Easton.

It is not so much that over a period of several years the family experienced extraordinary phenomena, although there was some of that, too. What distinguishes the Easton's home from the "ordinary" haunted house is the frequency of incidents, and the number of spectral beings that have caused them. As Culbertson noted in a front page article in 1989, the couple and their children had to share their place with a "battalion of noisy, sometimes nasty spirits."

The events began even before the Easton's moved into the house in 1967. A month before they took occupancy, they were moving some furniture and sat down downstairs to take a break. Both Bill and Marie heard footsteps upstairs, in a set pattern; four steps forward, then four back. There was no one else at home. When the footsteps repeated, the couple left for the night. After moving in, this phenomena reoccurred a number of times, but a source for the sounds was never found. One evening Marie heard someone call her name. She walked into the front room and asked Bill what he wanted. He told her he hadn't said a word. On other occasions, it appeared as if the spirits in the house wanted to help keep things cleaned. The dishwasher would start up by itself, and the vacuum cleaner did, too.

In 1972, when the Easton's daughter was two-and-a-half-years old, she told her parents that she had two friends, named Mark and

---

C H A P T E R   3 2

Strange Guests at the 'Ghost Hotel'

air raising noises in the dead of night . . . bone-chilling apparitions and ectoplasmic manifestations". . .all part of a "spectral vortex". . . at Augusta County's "Ghost Hotel." This is how Waynesboro News-Virginian reporter Charles Culbertson described the 240-year-old brick mansion west of Staunton owned by Bill and Marie Easton.

It is not so much that over a period of several years the family experienced extraordinary phenomena, although there was some of that, too. What distinguishes the Easton's home from the "ordinary" haunted house is the frequency of incidents, and the number of spectral beings that have caused them. As Culbertson noted in a front page article in 1989, the couple and their children had to share their place with a "battalion of noisy, sometimes nasty spirits."

The events began even before the Easton's moved into the house in 1967. A month before they took occupancy, they were moving some furniture and sat down downstairs to take a break. Both Bill and Marie heard footsteps upstairs, in a set pattern; four steps forward, then four back. There was no one else at home. When the footsteps repeated, the couple left for the night. After moving in, this phenomena reoccurred a number of times, but a source for the sounds was never found. One evening Marie heard someone call her name. She walked into the front room and asked Bill what he wanted. He told her he hadn't said a word. On other occasions, it appeared as if the spirits in the house wanted to help keep things cleaned. The dishwasher would start up by itself, and the vacuum cleaner did, too.

In 1972, when the Easton's daughter was two-and-a-half-years old, she told her parents that she had two friends, named Mark and

Amy. They were invisible, but the daughter played with them as if they were real. It was at about this time that Marie told a parapsychologist about the strange happenings at her house. He suggested a seance be held to see is he could root out the causes of the ghostly appearances.

A medium was brought in and "made contact" with the spirit of an old Black nanny who was "upset over the death of her young mistress." The mistress apparently had fallen in love with a young man who rode off to fight in the Civil War and never returned. The mistress "grieved" herself to death, and the nanny went to her own grave grieving for the mistress.

Further probing by the medium unveiled that the young man had died in a fierce battle and his "remains were charred beyond recognition. "The soldier's name, the medium said, was Mark and his lover's name was Amy. At that, Bill Easton "bolted out of his chair." Mark and Amy were the names of the imaginary friends of his daughter. "The hair stood up on the back of my neck," he was quoted as saying. "There was no way the medium - or anyone - could have known about my daughters invisible friends, and the odds of coming up with those two particular names were astronomical."

Later in the seance, the medium said the nanny said there were many ghosts in the house. In the weeks and months afterwards, more manifestations surfaced. Once, in the middle of the night, the family was shaken awake by an "enormous crash from downstairs." "This wasn't just a 'bump' in the night," Bill later said. "It sounded like someone took a tray full of dishes and slammed it on the floor." Bill and his teenage son searched "every corner and crevice of the house, but found not even a wine glass was out of place."

Another night, Bill was reading in bed when he heard a single note being played on the piano downstairs. No one in the family was downstairs. He got up and walked to the head of the stairs and listened as the note was played over and over. "I didn't even bother to go downstairs," he said. "I knew I wouldn't find anything, so I just went back to bed."

Most incidents were harmless, though perhaps a little scary. But then one night in the late 1980s, a ghost or ghosts seemed to turn mean. On a bitter winter night, Bill put the family dog in a room in the cellar to shield him from the cold. He locked the door from the inside with a heavy, 18th century sliding bolt. At midnight, the dog started howling uncontrollably, arousing Bill and Marie. Bill took a pistol and walked down to see what was the matter with the dog. When he entered the basement room, he found the sliding bolt had been thrown back, the door was standing open, and the dog had run outside.

He tried to coax the dog back into the house, but it wouldn't come, so Bill rebolted the door and went back to bed. The next morning, when Marie went to the basement to do some laundry, she found the cellar door open again, only this time the bolt had been shattered. "It was smashed to pieces," Bill said. "And this wasn't some flimsy sliding lock you buy at a hardware store. It was a huge, oaken bolt that would have taken an enormous amount of strength to shatter." An investigator from the Augusta County Sheriff's Department said it appeared the lock had been smashed from the inside.

And so it goes on. The guests at the ghost hotel continue their shenanigans. Bill and Marie Easton seem resigned to it. "When you live through 22 years of those things happening, you say 'what else is new?'" says Bill. "It's something we've lived with most of our adult lives, but it hasn't made us feel uncomfortable."

CHAPTER 3 3

Stone Showers from Hell

(Authors' note: Forget all the far-out fiction you may have seen in movies about poltergeists, leading to a vast array of Hollywood's most imaginative (and ugly) monsters, black pits of seemingly endless depths, extra-terrestrial type flights to another world and all that. Such fanciful nonsense has no semblance of relationship to the very real world of psychic phenomena. So cleanse your minds of any past remembrances of hideous, blood-covered creations snatching curly-haired little girls into the bottomless chasms of the beyond. It doesn't happen.

The German word poltergeist (from poltern — to knock) means "a noisy, usually mischievous ghost held to be responsible for unexplained noise (as rappings)." Poltergeists also long have been credited with the supernatural ability to move objects and throw things around on occasion. Some believe this is an angry type of ghost, and there have been cases where the manifestations have been abusive in nature. The notorious Bell Witch of Tennessee quickly comes to mind. In this well-documented case which occurred near Nashville in 1817, members of the Bell family were physically harassed by the spirit of a dead woman who believed she had been cheated by them. They were slapped, pinched, choked and haunted nearly out of their wits.

In "The Ghosts of Richmond and Nearby Environs," I wrote about an agitated poltergeist at the famous Dodson Tavern in Petersburg who "threw things around the house in fits of rage" which eventually attracted large crowds of witnesses. In this instance, books flew off shelves and across rooms, one hitting a workman in the chest. In "The Ghosts of Tidewater," I reported on the "return" of a mother from her watery grave to continually scold two teenage daughters who had disobeyed her. She allegedly even braided their pigtails together as they slept.

I also told of a house in Portsmouth where so many objects — from glass vases to tobacco cans — sailed from room to room, flung by unseen hands, that it became so dangerous the occupants had to move out. And there was another occurrence in Virginia Beach where a teenage girl, upset because her parents had grounded her, walked by her mother who was preparing soup in the kitchen. Eye witnesses swore the soup came out of the pot and soaked the mother.

Were all these incredible instances the work of poltergeists? Some experts believe not. They contend the flying objects and unexplained loud noises were, in reality, caused by human beings rather than ghosts, generally adolescent youths. They cite a phenomena known as Recurrent Spontaneous Psycho-kinesis, or RSPK. Dr. William G. Roll is a nationally known and respected scientist who has studied RSPK for decades. He says, "our focus on such eruptions has been on the individual who is at the center of the disturbances," which he concludes are sparked by tension or certain neurological features.

Another expert, Dr. Helmut Schmidt, former director of the Institute for Parapsychology in Durham, North Carolina, has written extensively on the subject. He sees a consistent pattern in the agents Dr. Roll has examined. "Poltergeist agents usually have a low ability at verbal expression," he has written. "This is coupled with built-up hostility that is being repressed from consciousness. These agents seem to be persons who have a deep feeling of hostility and frustration, and a crippling inability to express this hostility." Dr. Schmidt believes that often the person involved, such as the daughter in the soup incident, tries to repress such feelings in the hidden regions of their unconscious, therefore they may be unaware they are actually causing an action. To this, Dr. Roll adds that the thrown objects seem to indicate that some "moving force field or vortex" is responsible.

It is an intriguing dilemma. Can the human mind affect the outside world by pure thought? Dr. Schmidt says this question has captured our imagination throughout the ages, and he summarizes that during the last half century, careful laboratory world "has shown that man can, to a certain degree, influence the outside world by pure thought." But he also points out that the "psychologically induced RSPK explanation cannot fully explain all the manifestations of the poltergeist. He warns, too, that while significant breakthroughs have been made in the psychological study of the poltergeist, the poltergeist has not yet been explained nor has its actual mechanisms been explored. He admits the door to the eventual understanding of such phenomena may have been opened, but there is still much to learn before the full mysteries of poltergeists can be understood.

And so the question remains today. Are the actions of poltergeists triggered by ghosts from the past or by those who were living at the time? Was the mother's pot of soup spilled by her angry teenage daughter or by the unseen hands of a spirit who was sympathetic to the daughter?

All of this is a prelude to the following account of one of the most bizarre and celebrated cases of poltergeist activity on record. In fact, one of the nation's leading experts of extra-sensory perception and supernatural manifestations has called the *McChesney Ghost* "one of the five authentic poltergeists in the U.S.," to which no natural explanation can be given. One of the first major accounts of this extraordinary phenomena was given in the "Annals of Augusta County, Virginia from 1726 to 1871" by Joseph Waddell, a member of the Virginia Historical Society. While this activity occurred over a two year period beginning in 1825, it is still talked about in the area and has been passed down from generation to generation by the descendants of Dr. John McChesney and Thomas Steel, many of whom still live in the Staunton area west of Charlottesville.

Even the Conservative Virginia Historic Landmarks Commission, in its usually stilted architectural survey form outlining the McChesney house noted, "This is the house known locally as the Haunted House. Before the War Between the States, it was the scene of tongs dancing on the hearth, fire and brimstone raining down, etc."

The following account was taken from many sources, including the recollections of William Steele, son of Thomas, who in 1889 was one of the last surviving witnesses of what had happened. It was at that time, at age 70, that he told of what he had witnessed in the 1820s when he was a child of six. In the 1950s, Margaret McChesney was the last living link between the time of the occurrences and the present. She then was in her nineties, and had heard the story first-hand both from her aunt, Amanda, and from Dr. McChesney himself, her grandfather. Despite her advanced age, she maintained an exceptionally keen and alert mind, and she had said that someday the "last of the McChesneys" would tell the entire story that had never been known outside the family. For it was said that only the family knew the whole story, and it was a subject upon which they maintained an unbroken silence for well over a century. This is so, because even Waddell's well researched report did not include some of the strangest — and saddest — details.

When her sister died, Margaret became the last of the

McChesneys to know the complete story, and in 1954, when she was 92, she dictated it to her niece, Evelyn Jones Yarbrough. As one newspaper reporter later wrote, "Why would a woman on her death bed record such a tale? She had nothing to gain, surely, and neither did the distinguished family. There is no other explanation except it is the truth."

This is the story.)

Dr. McChesney has been described as an "intelligent physician" who lived on his farm in a house called Greenwood about a mile north of the village of Newport in Augusta County just off the main road leading from Staunton to Lexington He was, "a respected physician, a stern but just man, and a staunch Presbyterian." He lived a busy, well-ordered life, and was accustomed to having his word and his wishes obeyed without question. His wife was a sister of Thomas Steele (William's father) who lived about a mile away. Mrs. Mary Steele, widow of Captain William Steele and the mother of Thomas and Mrs. McChesney, lived in Rockbridge, two miles west of Midway.

Then, Dr. McChesney's family consisted of his wife and four young children. A prosperous man, he owned a number of slaves. Among them was a girl named Maria who was, at the time, around 12 years old. And it began with Maria — the first episode that was to lead to total disruption of the peaceful, orderly life at Greenwood.

It was, as Margaret McChesney recounted, "a warm spring afternoon. In the kitchen the servants were busy with preparations for the evening meal. Mrs. McChesney was seated in a chair in the parlor rocking her infant son, James, when the quiet was pierced by loud screams from the yard. Almost immediately, Maria burst into the room obviously terrified and screaming that an old woman with her 'head tied up' had beaten and chased her. Mrs McChesney, trying to soothe both Maria and James, could see that there were welts and bruises on the girl, but could make no sense out of what Maria was saying about the old woman. Finally she lost patience and ordered Maria out of the room.

"Soon Mrs. McChesney succeeded in quieting James and rocking him to sleep. Then she heard the tinkle of glasses in the nearby dining room. A decanter of wine and some wine glasses stayed on the tray on the sideboard and the house slaves were known to get into the wine whenever an opportunity presented itself. So, thinking to catch the culprit, Mrs. McChesney, still holding the baby, crept

softly to the dining room door. The room was empty, but the tray with the decanter and bottles intact had been pushed so far to the edge of the sideboard that only the rim rested against the board. Yet it was perfectly level. . . simply hanging there in mid-air defying every natural law.

"Dumbfounded, Mrs. McChesney returned the tray to its proper place and returned to the parlor. Promptly, the tinkle of wine glasses could be heard in the dining room, and when she went back, the tray again was suspended in the air with its rim barely touching the sideboard.

"The months of misery had begun.

"Now began a steady barrage of clods and mud and rocks hurled through the house and in the yard. Sometimes they came from *inside the house*, sometimes from the outside, yet no one could determine where they came from and they followed no directional pattern. Often, the rocks were hot and actually singed the spots where they fell, and they left great dents in the furniture.

"Maria was the special target for abuse. Frequently, the girl would go into convulsive screaming fits crying that she was being beaten. The sounds of heavy slaps and blows could be heard distinctly above her cries, and, before the eyes of the members of the family, great welts would appear on her body."

While the children found some of these "peculiarities" amusing and exciting, and Mrs. McChesney was "extremely perturbed," Dr. McChesney pronounced the whole affair "utter nonsense" and refused to discuss it or allow anyone to mention it to him.

Margaret McChesney continued with her remembrances: "Before events got really serious, the children and some cousins decided it would be a great idea to have a table seance and try to contact whatever it was that kept throwing things around the house. Into this gleeful gathering came the doctor, and he was outraged to find members of his family solemnly trying to establish contact with a spook. In terms so stern that his daughter Amanda never forgot them, he berated them for their sinful ways and ordered that there never again be any talk of ghosts in his home. For his decisive stand, he was promptly showered with clods and mud pelted him from every direction. Incredibly, he chose to ignore this!"

In succeeding weeks, the volleys of stones continued, thundering down on the roof of the house in broad daylight as well as at night. One writer said, "sometimes they came thickly, like a barrage of gunfire, sometimes only one at a time, and hours apart. It is said the stones averaged "the size of a man's fist," and some of them were "too large to be thrown by a person of ordinary strength." Not once, during any of the incidents, was anyone seen hurling stones at the house.

Word of the strange and ominous events at Greenwood started to seep through the countryside, and curiosity seekers began arriving. This, said Margaret McChesney, "was a bitter blow to Dr. McChesney and soon he abandoned all attempts to be courteous and drove strangers away the minute he set eyes on them. One day a man arrived at the front door which, by chance, was opened by the doctor. The stranger announced that he had heard from someone in Richmond of the occurrences at Greenwood so he had come to stay awhile and make an investigation of the phenomena. Dr. McChesney wrathfully retorted that he would be glad to have him stay provided the man would tell him the name of the damn fool in Richmond who had the idea Greenwood was a hotel." (The family thought this incident was particularly humorous, because the doctor never swore in their presence.)

And still they came! Even in that day of sluggish travel and poor communications, the work continued to spread throughout an ever-expanding area. Literally hundreds of people from miles around travelled to the farm to see the "devil's handiwork" for themselves. Some were rewarded, some were not, because the stones did not fall everyday. Along with the curious came the crackpots offering all kinds of unsought and unheeded advice. Even the doctor's vigilance and righteous indignation failed to keep them away.

There is one report that a group of church elders from one of the nearby towns ventured to the McChesney farm. They were cordially received, but when the subject of the stones was brought up "a shadow crossed the doctor's face." The men were invited to dinner, and according to the legend, as one of them reached for a biscuit, a sharp black stone flew from a corner of the ceiling across the room and sliced the biscuit in half!

It was during this period that a frightened Mrs. McChesney pleaded with her husband to move, but he adamantly refused, contending that "no intelligent person could believe for one minute that his home had been invaded by ghosts." Stubbornly, he stuck to the firm assumption that as long as he refused to admit anything was wrong, everything was bound to be all right.

Margaret McChesney continued: "Mrs. McChesney was increasingly aware that the bulk of the disturbances seemed to center around Maria, the young slave girl. The beatings were more frequent, more severe. During one of them, Maria screamed that 'the old woman with her head tied up' was demanding that Maria give her a white lacey shawl belonging to Mrs. McChesney. Despite her anxiety, Mrs. McChesney firmly refused to give the shawl to a malicious unseen character who was making their lives so miserable.

"On another occasion, Maria, in a whining petulant mood, was hanging around the kitchen getting in everybody's way and complaining that she was hungry. Finally, she became such a nuisance that the cook shoved her out the door. While the girl stood crying on the back porch, she was fiercely pelted with large floppy objects that appeared to be soggy oversized pancakes. Members of the family, hastily summoned by the servants, saw and handled these objects.

"During one of the flying rock episodes, a large rock was thrown into the pitcher. This pitcher had a broad rounded base and a long narrow neck — the neck impossibly small for a rock of that size to pass through without shattering it. But the rock was there — almost covering the bottom of the pitcher — and there it stayed for many, many years."

Now the harassment took a sinister turn. The baby James began to have strange and frightening seizures. Lying in his crib one day, he suddenly went into a screaming fit, and what appeared to be tiny bloody pinpricks spread rapidly across his body." Mrs. McChesney demanded that something be done, and the doctor reluctantly agreed to send Maria away — to the home of his brother-in-law.

"Brother-in-law and his family, in total ignorance of the proposed visit from Maria, were seated on the lawn entertaining guests when from inside the house, came the clatter of horses hooves — indeed, it sounded like a stampede. Rushing into the house, they found that every stick of furniture and all the knickknacks in the parlor had been piled in the middle of the floor. While they stared in disbelief, clods and rocks began to sail through the room and crash into the furniture. Panic-stricken, they rushed outside and saw Maria approaching the house. She was immediately sent back to Greenwood!

"Following this, the beatings of Maria were intensified . . . night and day the rocks and clods of mud sailed through the house and yard. . . and James' seizures grew more frequent and more terrifying. One day Mrs. McChesney, rocking her son, was badly shaken when a chair, which was placed sedately against the wall, 'walked' across the room and came to rest beside her. Hastily, she moved to the other side of the room, and when the chair followed her, she became hysterical and ran screaming from the house, still clutching her child.

"It seems incredible that Dr. McChesney still could not bring himself to acknowledge that he and his family were up against something that defied reason or explanation. To him the very question of a ghost was both a sin and a disgrace, and he had no intention of giving in. Convinced that he, a physician, could cure the baby of whatever was afflicting him, he refused to leave Greenwood or seek outside help.

"While the doctor tried with all his medical skill and knowledge to cure his son, the seizures increased and with each one James grew weaker. And finally he died in the convulsive throes of a screaming fit while his tiny body flamed with the bloody pinpricks.

"Only then did the stunned, grieving doctor face the harsh fact that he had so long tried to ignore: that some terrible and evil force had been unleashed in their lives.

"The day of the baby's funeral, after the family had returned from the cemetery, Amanda and some cousins were standing on the front porch near the open door. From inside the house came the by now all-too-familiar thuds of rocks and clods being hurled against the furniture. In a reckless frenzy of rage and grief, Amanda stepped through the doorway and screamed, Consarn ye! Why don't you pick on somebody old enough to fight back?' Immediately, from inside the house, came a large rock which struck her in the forehead cutting a long deep gash. The injury was so severe that she carried the scar for the rest of her life. Although many people were hit by mud and rocks, Amanda was the only person injured by one of the flying rocks."

Indignant, Thomas Steele cursed the "invisible agent" for taking its spite on a woman and not him. He then sat defiantly in the front door, and instantly was "pelted with clods of sod and earth, coming from the inside of the house." He sat until he was almost covered with "missiles piled around him, moving only after his mother screamed that "the thing" would kill him.

Fearing for the safety of his family, Dr. McChesney moved his children to their grandmother's house near Midway. Maria went, too. Soon, the disturbances began in this house, with some new variations. Stones flew about and furniture in the kitchen "moved of its own accord." One day a large kitchen bench "pranced over the floor like a horse." The children thought this was funny, and one of them said he was going to ride the bucking bronco, but he became so alarmed that he fainted. Nor were the manifestations limited to the house itself. Farm hands said that food and tools were "taken by them to the fields disappeared." They turned up in the house.

Aunt Lucy Anderson, an old slave who lived and worked at the farm during this time was quoted as saying she had gone into the wine closet under the stairway in the hall one day and saw the bottles "turn upside down and start dancing with nobody near them." She also told of benches that "walked by themselves" on the porch.

At Mrs. Steele's house, Maria complained of being beaten by unseen hands. Mrs. Steele took the girl between her knees, drew her skirts up and struck all around Maria with a stick "as if to beat off an invisible foe." Maria then cried out that she was being pricked with pins and slapped. William Steele said the slaps could be distinctly heard, but "no one could see the vindictive enemy." Finally, Marie fell in exhaustion to the floor, "apparently dead." She was soon revived, but she continued to be punished by her ghostly tormenter.

All of this — the death of her infant son, the stoning of Amanda, and the continuing blitz of clods and rocks and other inexplicable occurrences — was too much for Mrs. McChesney. She told the doctor if he wouldn't move she would leave without him. As a last resort, Dr. McChesney sold Maria and her parents, sending them away forever. From that day on, the disturbances stopped and never reoccurred. The doctor and his family subsequently moved to

Staunton, and he refused, for the rest of this life, to discuss the poltergeist activities.

The whole affair is considered psychically important for a couple of reasons. One, the family was known as one of respectability and prominence, and the McChesneys were much embarrassed by the occurrences and were reluctant to talk about them. Secondly, the incidents were eye witnessed by scores of credible people over an extended period of time.

Was the phenomenon caused by the young girl herself? Was she unhappy in her surroundings, and venting her wrath by means of psycho-kinesis? Or were she and the McChesney and Steele families being taunted by a vicious spirit who used Maria as the medium for the malicious actions, avenging some past offense? Or could there be yet a third explanation? William Steele said that there was an "old Negro woman: who lived in the neighborhood and "walked with a stick and chewed tobacco." William apparently feared the woman because he said that in his boyhood he always was careful "to give her the road when they met." Maria, who had a reputation for having "an evil tongue," was said to have sassed the woman and in return was threatened with punishment. William added that the old woman was reputed to be a witch. Had she cast a spell on Maria?

A report on Greenwood by the Virginia Historic Landmarks Commission stated "it was thought that a little Black slave girl, who complained of pins and needles sticking her, may have been the source of the problem. For when she was sold to the south all the occurrences stopped. However, others in the community thought that the house was bewitched. Still others in the area asserted that the owners (McChesneys) were cruel to their slaves, and that this was the slaves method of retaliation."

And, finally, there is this footnote. More than half a century ago Margaret F. Wade wrote a prize-winning story about the McChesney ghost. She claimed the phenomena actually started at the near-simultaneous births of Maria to Aunt Liza in the slave quarters and Ellen McChesney in the "big house." She wrote: "A gust of wind shattered a window and swept out the lights in the farmhouse near Brownsburgh, and large rocks fell at Dr. John McChesney's feet, while in the slaves' quarters, the wind was so strong it turned Aunt Liza's bed completely around."

The deep questions involved here likely will never be satisfactorily answered. But from witnesses who said they saw the stones fall, and from the first-hand testimony of William Steele, there is little doubt that something very strange occurred in Augusta County,

Virginia, in 1825. They still talk about it today.

When Elizabeth Sterrett wrote about the phenomena, telling what she had been told by the 92-year-old Margaret McChesney, she said to a newspaper interviewer, "Perhaps this article and the work of the Augusta County Historical Society might not only free the McChesney name from ridicule, but once and for all the truth can conquer the legend of the McChesney Ghost.

"It was real and it was evil and no one will ever know exactly what it was."

* * * * *

Incredulous as it seems, a strikingly similar occurrence of stone showers from Hell apparently occurred at Greenwood, a manor house that, curiously, was built near Culpepper at about the same time the McChesneys were being bedeviled on their farm. It was built for John Williams Green, a judge of the Virginia Supreme Court, and has been described as having a "pleasing but unpretentious formality." Here, in 1825, Judge Green received the Marquis de Lafayette and former President James Monroe during Lafayette's celebrated tour as "guest of the nation."

At some point in time in the 19th century — the date is not clear — a plantation overseer named Edwards and his wife lived in a dependent house at Greenwood. When they died, a "colored family" moved in. Shortly after that, the Negro tenant came to the owner of the house and complained that he couldn't live there anymore because "Mrs. Edwards threw stones at them!" He reported that "showers of stones," some of considerable size, would at times fall from the ceiling, enter through the windows, and "come out of the walls, zigzagging across the room." Some of the stones were wet, while others were hot.

The owners at first, of course, did not believe. But they, too, witnessed the eerie phenomena, and soon, as with the McChesney incident, people from all over the county came "in buggies, dearborns or on horseback" to see the remarkable demonstrations. Many believed it to be the devil's work, striking fear through the medium of the Negro family. They determined to root out the cause.

And so they came, one day. A small army of self-proclaimed crusaders, each armed with a pistol or a rifle. They entered the house and lined up the family members, telling them if anyone moved they would be shot on the spot! It is said that within minutes, as the Negroes stood stock still a barrage of stones rained down from the ceiling upon the "investigators," who abruptly and unceremoniously departed in extreme haste. Soon after, the house was torn down to the ground.

It was not recorded whether or not the Negro family had a child of Maria's age.

* * * * *

Case histories of the phenomena of hurling stones actually go back more than a thousand years. In the year 858, for example, the German town of Bingen-on-the-Rhine was pelted with rocks. In 1592, stones weighing as much as 20 pounds apiece rained down on a farm in Oxfordshire, England. And there have been more recent reports of such manifestations. In 1962, a family living in Big Bear City, California, suffered through a four-month-long barrage of rocks and pebbles. In all of these instances, as with the McChesney occurrences, no satisfactory answer to the cause was ever forthcoming. Perhaps the best reply came from a French gendarme who investigated a stone incident in Paris in 1846. "Whence came these projectiles," he said, "from their weight and the distance they are hurled, are clearly from no mortal hand!"

It should be noted, too, that on the night of July 11, 1682, the New Hampshire home of George Walton and his family was stoned from all directions, although an investigation failed to reveal any human agent for the flurries, which lasted several days. The secretary for the province of New Hampshire, Richard Chamberlain, came to witness the scene, and was himself struck several times. He concluded that the stonings "must necessarily be done by means extraordinary and preternatural." It is said, too, that Increase Mather and his son, Cotton Mather, used this widely publicized affair to persuade skeptics of the reality of the supernatural. They also used it to further their firm belief in the "real existence of apparitions, spirits and witches." Ten years later the Mathers were instrumental in the famous Salem, Massachusetts, witch hunts.

Dark Tragedy at Belnemus

t is such a charming spot, so intimately wel-
coming that you could not believe that there
was the scene of one of the most bloodcurdling ghost stories that
ever raised your knotted and combined locks heavenward. But the
ghost story — as you read it — seems such a likely story that much
as you'd like to, you cannot find a single reason for doubting it . . .
.You tell yourself that it all happened so long ago, 130 years ago, but
you look around quickly and those icy fingers seem to grip you so
that you can do nothing but swallow hard and wish for the light of
day."

This is how Margaret Barker Seward wrote about the 200-year-
old Powhatan County plantation known as Belnemus in a special
article published in the Richmond Times-Dispatch Magazine in May
1939. She quoted from a book, "In Our Country — Stories of Old
Virginia Life," written by the noted Virginia author Marion Harland,
a native Powhatan, published in 1901. It certainly has all the elements of a classic tale of melancholy and hauntings: a beautiful
young woman, unhappily linked to a wicked older man with a cruel
countenance and appearance; a brutal murder; and the apparitional
return of both the victim and villain. There is a discrepancy as to
when Belnemus, which means "beautiful wood," was built, and for
whom. Ms. Seward said the house, located in the Powhatan
Courthouse vicinity between Richmond and Charlottesville, was
constructed in 1760 by the Mayo family. One of the Mayo ancestors
is said to have walked about in the falls of Richmond with William
Byrd II when he was laying out the city. According to the Virginia
Landmarks Register, however, Belnemus was erected between 1783
and 1799 for "James Clarke, a Powhatan County landowner and
politician, on land purchased from Col. William Mayo."

Through the centuries the house has been altered to include a big
front porch with pillars and "countless side porches with roses

climbing up their columns." The main house was flanked by a smokehouse and a dairy. "Inside the smoke house," Ms. Seward wrote, "you smell the matchless smell of Virginia bacon and ham, and, if you look upward you can see far into the darkness countless sides of bacon and hams suspended as if in mid-air. To the old Virginian it is as beautiful a sight as a star-studded sky."

Upon entering the mansion, she added, "you find yourself in as charming a room as you could hope to see; for at the right there is a great fireplace with a most beautiful mantel." The mantel was once described by a staff member of the Metropolitan Museum of New York as a "splendid and interesting example of early American woodwork," Above the fireplace, said Ms. Seward, were some "lovely ornaments which look to be fleurs de lys. . . for the home was built by a Huguenot family, and Powhatan County was the seat of the first Huguenot settlement in the New World."

There also were, at one time, three thriving mills at Belnemus Plantation, and all three worked overtime during the War Between the States grinding corn for the Confederate armies. But the ghost story precedes this era by perhaps 60 years. As best can be determined, the ethereal events occurred probably sometime late in the first decade of the 19th century. The following account is pieced together from the writings of Ms. Seward, Marion Harland, and other faded recollections.

Sometime after the turn of the 19th century, the plantation had come up for sale. It had been for a time owned by the Scott family, and both Colonel Scott and his older brother, "Wild Jim" Scott, had garnered reputations as "hardened old sinners who drank hard, gambled freely, and often fought over women." There had been six Scott brothers in all and only one had died a natural death. One had fallen in the War of 1812, two had been killed "out West," and two, including Wild Jim, had committed suicide.

Young Burr Mayo bought the house and planned to move into it with his bride-to-be, Lucy Flournoy. Shortly after the purchase, Mayo and two friends inspected the old house. They were surprised to find, in a drawing room, a massive sofa which stood against the front wall near the fireplace. There, too, was a "cloudy mirror," and six chairs, heavy and claw-footed like the sofa. They had presumed that most if not all the furnishings had been sold at an auction following Colonel Scott's death. In a cubby in the attic, the men found two unframed portraits with "the dust of an unknown number of years caked upon them." After some considerable cleaning, they discovered that one was of a beautiful girl with large eyes, while the other was of a man with "a cruel, sensual mouth." Mayo later shoved the pictures back into the cubby and forgot about them.

Soon after, as carpenters, painters and furnishers worked in the house, Mayo began sleeping there at night to keep current with the progress of the restoration. He was to say later that he slept there for two months and "never saw or heard anything unusual or unnatural. Indeed, the premises were too quiet. . . everything was so deadly still."

Then, one August, as he slept on the curious old couch he was aroused by "the touch of something cold upon his hand thrown over his head upon the pillow." He awoke instantly, and was to say the coldness upon his hand was "a creepy sensation as if dead fingers had clasped his." He then heard a "movement" at the far end of the darkened room, near the door. He had locked the door and bolted the Venetian shutters of the windows before going to bed. He said the movement was a step, slow and irregular — the tread of a human creature. It passed to the head of the room on the opposite side from him, then down again, keeping the same distance away, pacing back and forth. The feet, Mayo felt, were unshod, either stocking or naked. At first he thought it might be a prowling thief, but then he wasn't sure. There was something very strange about this "presence."

Mayo slowly rose to his feet, as the footsteps continued to pace about. Next, the mystery walker reached the antique sofa, and, as Mayo was to relate, "a heavy body fell upon it with a force that made it tremble and creak," With the fall came a "deep human groan and a horrible gurgle." Then all was still. Though terrified, Mayo managed to light a candle. He looked down at the sofa where he had heard the body fall and the "life blood gush from his throat." There was nothing there! Nor was there anything anywhere in the room. It was 20 minutes past 2 a.m., and Mayo's heart "beat like a trip-hammer; his tongue dried within his mouth."

He resolved not to tell his fiance about the encounter until he could find a rational explanation for it. The next day he decided to interrogate a 90-year-old slave who had lived all his life at the plantation and might well know of past dark deeds associated with it. He asked "Uncle Cumby" if he had ever heard of the great house being haunted. The old timer, after all, told fortunes, and "was supposed to understand certain magical arts." Mayo suggested to him that the ghost might have been that of Wild Jim Scott who "blew out his brains or cut his throat." Maybe, the young owner said, "he is sent back as part of his punishment for the deeds done in the flesh." But Cumby, whose bleared eyes "had an evil gleam," wouldn't discuss

the matter, and, in fact, seemed agitated at the questioning.

Mayo courageously continued to sleep in the downstairs room, but over the next two months, nothing happened. With his wedding 10 days off, he had the old sofa, which he called "hideous," taken up to the attic for storage. It took six men to do the job. It was in the attic that Burr Mayo noticed the dark stain at one end of the couch. It was irregular in shape and ran to outer edge of the seat. He believed it to be a bloodstain.

Sometime in the next week Lucy Flournoy, her sister, and a friend were poking around in the attic when they, too, discovered the aging, dusty portraits in the cubby. They noticed the girl with "large, lustrous eyes," had a profusion of waving black hair looped about a tall carved comb, and a rich brunette complexion. Her skin was like "clear coffee." Her neck and shoulders were bare but for a necklace of gold beads. Her lips were full. The three women speculated that she had once been a belle. There was, too, something inexplicably "familiar" about her to Lucy. Lucy couldn't quite put her finger on it, but the portrait stirred a strange feeling. They all cringed at the man's portrait. One of them said, "he has the evilest eyes I ever beheld!"

Dying of curiosity, Lucy had the same idea as Mayo. She decided to call upon Uncle Cumby to clear up the mystery as to the identities of the portraits. But when she showed the pictures to the old man, he reacted violently, raising a cane above his head in a threatening manner, his face "hideous with rage." Frightened and mystified, Lucy ran from his cabin. She told Mayo about her experience and said she wanted to go back to Cumby and try again. He was dead set against this and they argued heatedly.

That night the moon was full and all was quiet. Mayo was out walking across the upper garden when he saw who he thought was Lucy sneaking down toward Cumby's house. He could hardly believe she had defied his wishes. A white shawl was draped around her head and shoulders and he couldn't see her face. What he saw was a "fleeting figure. . .going so fast with a light, skimming motion, more like the flight of a bird than the walk of a woman." She sped down the garden slope, "slipped through the gate, and glided on, like a wind-driven mist, across the wheat field until she turned the corner of Cumby's cabin." Mayo followed her until he got to the gate. Then his mouth dropped open in astonishment. The latch was so stiff with rust, the wood of the gate so swollen by recent rains, that all his strength was required to raise the one side and push the other. Yet the "vision" he was chasing had not hesitated at the gate. She had drifted through it as if it wasn't there!

Mayo stalked back to the main house rehearsing the severe tongue lashing he planned to give his disobedient bride, only to find her sewing by the hearth! She was wearing a crimson dress. The figure he had followed had been clad in gray! Mayo was "speechless and confounded." Lucy told him she had not left the house. Who then had he seen?

That night, Lucy and Mayo went back to the attic. As he was shoving the portraits deep into the cubby, Lucy was standing by an old trunk. Suddenly, she screamed, "Oh, Burr, dear! Don't" He looked around in time to see her topple backward and fall, striking her head on the floor. He quickly grabbed her and lifted her up. She was nearly hysterical. "Why did you pull me over?" she yelled. "You gripped my neck and jerked me backward." "It wasn't me," he responded incredulously. "I wasn't within 10 feet of you." "Then who did?" she said. "I felt two cold hands about my neck as plainly as I feel your warm hands now. And you saw how hard I fell! It pulled me down!"

The next day Mayo had the ominous old couch taken down from the attic. He took it outside and burned it.

The following February, Lucy's cousin Bolling Flournoy visited the house and he and Mayo were downstairs in the room where the ghostly manifestations had occurred a few months earlier. There was a terrible storm outside, and rare winter flashes of lightening streaked through the sky. By a "simultaneous impulse they could never explain," both Bolling and Mayo turned around and looked behind them.

As Marion Harland wrote: "In the middle of the room, halfway between the hearth and the closed door, stood a woman, her arms raised over her head in prayer, or in imprecation." Mayo, in an instant, recognized the upturned face. The woman then "sank upon her hands, and, like one crouching under a blow, her shoulders shaking with sobs, she swept to the door — and was *not!*" Both men were stunned into silence. They instantly realized that the apparition had not opened the door! It was shut and fast when she disappeared beyond it. "The blood chilled and settled about the stout young hearts."

Then they heard a shrill shriek. They bounded to the door, opened it, and ran into the pitch-black hall. They heard a shuffle of feet, the rustle of garments, and short, loud breaths at the head of the stairs. Something fell — "rolling down! down! down! rebounding from each oaken stair, until a dull thud at the bottom ended the viewless tragedy." Mayo ran and got a candle only to find the hall and staircase vacant. As Lucy and the others were out of the house, they searched it from top to bottom and found nothing. Yet the front and back doors were locked and every window was fast shut. Mayo and Bolling then raced to the attic, and Mayo yanked the portrait of the beautiful girl out and showed it to Bolling. "That was who we saw," he shouted, and his companion agreed, saying, "I did, so help me Heaven!" The two men then ripped the canvas apart. Tacked behind the picture was a piece of paper pasted upon the wood. The paper was yellow-brown, but they could still read the ancient letters: "Daphne, 1802." They subsequently burned the portraits in a roaring fire.

The next morning, determined, Mayo went charging down to old Cumby's cabin. This time he would demand an answer to what tragedy had triggered the spate of ghostly phenomena. But he arrived to find that the elderly slave had died in his sleep that night. The gathered Negroes said they believed he had been killed by a thunderbolt! Mayo was aghast at the sight. "The head was strained back horribly; the lips, as black as an ape's, were drawn away from the toothless gums; mouth and eyes were open and too rigid to be closed."

Mayo and Bolling then swore a pack between them never to tell the story of the woman they had seen and her ill-fate. They swore never to relate what they strongly suspected — that Wild Jim Scott had, in a night of frenzy — murdered the dark-skinned woman, disposed of her, and then slit his own throat and collapsed on the old sofa. Mayo had all of Uncle Cumby's belongings burned in a pile, "bedding, furniture, clothing, and the nameless materials used in his unholy trade — feathers, bones, rabbit's feet, beads and scores of other things of no value except to the owner, who had known how to trick and conjure and bewitch with them."

That's when the hauntings stopped. Sometime later, Mayo decided to build a new tobacco barn on the site where Cumby's quarters had stood. In digging the foundation for this — as was vouched for by credible witnesses — "the workmen struck their spades into a human skeleton barely four feet below the surface. It was the skeleton of a woman of medium height, with straight slim limbs and a well-shaped head. There was no sign of a coffin to show that she had been decently interred." Rather, it appeared that she had been buried in haste. Lucy and Burr Mayo were summoned from the house. As they bent over the excavation, a Negro, cleaning the earth away from around the bones, "drew out and shook away the mould from a lock of silky black hair. Tangled in it was a tortoise-shell comb, high-backed and elaborately carved, such as Lucy had seen among her grandmother's treasures!"

The author, left, with his cousin, Layton Taylor, at Winton, the home of Patrick Henry's mother, in Amherst County.

About the Author

L. B. Taylor, Jr.—a Scorpio—is a native Virginian. He was born in Lynchburg and has a BS degree in Journalism from Florida State University. He wrote about America's space programs for 16 years, for NASA and aerospace contractors, before moving to Williamsburg, Virginia, in 1974, as public affairs director for BASF Corporation. He retired in 1993. Taylor is the author of more than 300 national magazine articles and 30 non-fiction books. His research for the book "Haunted Houses," published by Simon and Schuster in 1983, stimulated his interest in area psychic phenomena and led to the publication of five regional Virginia ghost books preceding "The Ghosts of Virginia."

(Personally autographed copies of: "The Ghosts of Williamsburg" — 84 pages, illustrated, $6; "The Ghosts of Richmond" — 172 pages, illustrated, $10; "The Ghosts of Tidewater" — 232 pages, illustrated, $11; "The Ghosts of Fredericksburg" — 177 pages, illustrated, $10; "The Ghosts of Charlottesville and Lynchburg" — 188 pages, illustrated, $10; and "The Ghosts of Virginia" — 401 pages, illustrated, $14 ($55 for all 6 books, $42 for the 5 regional books) are available from: L. B. Taylor, Jr., 248 Archer's Mead, Williamsburg, VA, 23185 (804-253-2636). Please add $2 shipping and handling charges for single book orders, $3 for more than one book. Also please specify to whom you wish the book(s) signed.)

OTHER BOOKS BY L. B. TAYLOR, JR.

PIECES OF EIGHT: Recovering the Riches of a Lost Spanish Treasure Fleet

THAT OTHERS MAY LIVE (Air Force Rescue & Recovery Service)

LIFTOFF: The Story of America's Spaceport

FOR ALL MANKIND

GIFTS FROM SPACE (Spinoff Benefits from Space Research)

CHEMISTRY CAREERS

SPACE SHUTTLE

RESCUE (True Stories of Teenage Heroism)

THE DRAFT

SHOPLIFTING

SPACE: BATTLEGROUND OF THE FUTURE

THE NUCLEAR ARMS RACE

THE NEW RIGHT

THE GHOSTS OF WILLIAMSBURG

SPOTLIGHT ON . . . (Four Teenage Idols)

EMERGENCY SQUADS

SOUTHEAST AFRICA

DRIVING HIGH (Effects of Alcohol and Drugs on Driving)

CHEMICAL AND BIOLOGICAL WARFARE

HAUNTED HOUSES

THE GHOSTS OF RICHMOND

THE COMMERCIALIZATION OF SPACE

ELECTRONIC SURVEILLANCE

HOSTAGE

THE GHOSTS OF TIDEWATER

THE GHOSTS OF FREDERICKSBURG